Living My tRuth

PERSONAL REFLECTIONS ON THE IMPACT OF THE RBG LEGACY

A Compilation By Cathy L. Davis

Living My tRuth
Personal Reflections on the Impact of the RBG Legacy
UpsiDaisy Press

Cover and Interior Design: Davis Creative Publishing Partners, DavisCreative.com
Writing Coach and Editor: Kay Uhles, KayClarkUhles.com

Compilation by Cathy L. Davis
Living My tRuth: Personal Reflections on the Impact of the RBG Legacy

ISBN: 978-1-7347971-4-5 (paperback)
       978-1-7347971-5-2 (ebook)

2021

TABLE OF CONTENTS

CATHY L. DAVIS

Introduction

The RBG Impact

It was the 1950s. Ruth Bader Ginsburg graduated from Cornell University in 1954, finishing first in her class. After attending Harvard Law School as a new mom, she transferred and graduated from Columbia Law School in New York in 1959 (also first in her class). I was three years old with a thirteen-year-old brother and a fifteen-year-old sister. Our mother struggled with the stigma of being a newly-single, working mom.

In the mid-1960s I attended grade school in Tulsa, Oklahoma. Never one to be a math wiz, I remember asking my teacher for help on a math problem. After a few minutes of trying to help me, I heard the older male teacher say, "Never mind, honey—you won't need math when you grow up. Just be sure to marry someone who can do it for you."

In the early 1970s, we had Kent State. Watergate. Roe v. Wade. Vietnam. The male/female roles in our society had started to change, in spite of what my old math teacher believed. We were living in a changing world, and it was a very confusing time to be a female—especially for a female teen in America.

At age fifteen, I was the first female student "allowed" to take a drafting/architectural drawing class in my high school.

At age sixteen after "acing" the Red Cross lifeguard course and test, I was turned down over the phone (as in, sight-unseen) for a summer job because "We only hire male lifeguards."

At age seventeen, I was invited to attend Yale University, as one of the FIRST female incoming freshman.

I went to on to college (not Yale) in the mid-1970s. Little did I know that behind the scenes was a petite female firecracker, Ruth Bader Ginsburg, attorney at law, well on her way to making an impact on the societal landscape—busily creating the stepping stones used by many of us to get to where we are today.

RBG took the "sting" out of "interesting" and embedded a societal INTEREST in creating a level playing field in the workplace, in finance, and in daily living. Mutual respect between males and females had become a cultural undercurrent and women had gained the confidence to begin standing up for themselves.

Ruth Bader Ginsburg was more than a Supreme Court justice…she was a leading lady who left her mark on law, feminism, and everyday life. From gender equality and employment rights to the separation of church and state, RBG left her stamp of approval—or dissent—on our culture. After twenty-seven years serving as a justice on the Supreme Court, Ruth Bader Ginsburg died on September 18, 2020. Her legacy continues through the lives that countless Americans are able to live today.

The women authors in this book represent all walks of life and each shares her own unique perspective on how their lives were impacted by RBG. Honor yourself, Ruth Bader Ginsburg, and women across America as you read these inspiring stories of Living My tRuth.

CATHY L. DAVIS

Books are in Cathy's DNA and have always played a big role in her life. Cathy Davis believes we all have a story to tell and it is through our stories that we are able to find our voice, share our wisdom, and make a difference in the lives of others. Wisdom not shared is wisdom lost forever.

Cathy spent the bulk of her career as a Designer and Creative Director of Corporate Communications for a global financial institution, managing a team of 18 designers and print specialists.

Cathy founded Davis Creative, LLC in January of 2004 after corporate downsizing. What originally began as a boutique creative services agency, is now known as a sought-after publishing industry leader, providing concierge publishing services for authors throughout the US and several foreign countries.

cathy@daviscreative.com
www.linkedin.com/in/cathyldavis/
www.youtube.com/channel/UC5L1yOYzT0gPP-tXY02ltVA
www.facebook.com/DavisCreativeLLC

Why Can't I?

Ironically, you might have read my story here as a tale of "Ruth," the name my parents gave me at birth (but later changed). So, as I share my journey with you, I wonder…was I destined from a young age to champion women's equality? Was Ruth Bader Ginsburg?

My childhood was good as the second of seven children. For nine years, I was "Daddy's helper" and followed him around as his "stand-in son." I rejoiced when my only brother was born.

Early on, I vowed not to be stuck like my dear, smart Mom. She worked hard for our family, including her household responsibilities that included catching dust bunnies before they landed. Dad labored to provide enough money for our basics, but after work his desire to relax trumped teaming up with Mom who kept energized, going, and going 'til midnight. I did not understand why she accepted unfairness. But my parents agreed on traditional roles, got along, and Dad was enthusiastically involved in our family life.

While Ruth Bader Ginsburg was completing her law degree in 1959, I attempted self-empowerment by asking a fourth-grade teacher about a "D" on my artwork. I called it "modern art" and "A" work. She called it "sloppy" and me impudent*—a word I looked up that night. I continued challenging school and church authority. Why can't I be a school patrol boy or altar boy? Where were the girls' soccer teams?

"Girls aren't allowed to" was the dumb answer they gave. Gender barriers were nonsense to me. I shrugged and pressed onward.

At 16, I pushed back vigorously when told typing class was <u>required only</u> for girls. (Did you know office work was a "backup support plan for girls" until they married?) I insisted I was never going to be anyone's secretary. Authority caved. I dropped typing. (School advisors never suggested I might regret lacking typing ability later when completing my doctoral dissertation and writing books.) I played on our area's first women's soccer team at 18 in games tagged "exhibition" and "powder puff." Our sponsoring tire company provided our practice field on the flat tar <u>roof</u> of their store.

After years of "playing teacher" to five younger sibs, I wanted to be a teacher. Following my plan, I completed an undergraduate degree and teaching certificate; but the education job market was glutted. Instead, I was hired as one of the first few female probation/parole officers in my state and proudly participated in stereotype busting. I gained respect from colleagues and my predominantly male caseload. During my second year, our governor handed me a "state probation officer of the year" plaque during a public ceremony.

After two years of state service, I was <u>specifically hired to be the female "replacement"</u> for the first female appointed as a US Probation Officer for the US District Court for the Eastern District of Missouri (USDC/EDMO). She resigned after a year to stay home with her newborn. I started my new job confidant about being the only female probation officer, an employee of that federal court district.

The Civil Rights Act passed eleven years prior to my 1975 appointment as a US Probation Officer. "Sexual harassment" became part of sex discrimination with a federal sexual harassment case in in 1976. Although I did not realize the name for it then, sexual harassment was active from the beginning on my job. I lunched daily with my all-male colleagues. One day at a pizza parlor with long tables and bench seating, the topic was "children". Learning I had none, one guy shouted, "Well, jump up on the table. We'll all get you started!" They laughed while I shrunk into humiliation and powerlessness. I remained silent.

There were incessant compliments regarding my appearance. Once, when I gathered enough courage, I replied "thanks" but informed him I'd rather be commended for my intelligence. He said little thereafter. One man (appointed supervisor instead of me) openly shared with male colleagues the porn magazines kept in his desk. A few men snuck up on me in the halls, plucked and snapped my bra crying out "Robin Hood!" One male officer became infuriated with a judge and kicked a hole in his office wall. Do you see anything unprofessional in this work climate?

Grown equally from desire and necessity, I got along with my male peers. My husband and I socialized with a group of them and their wives. As a 20-something who loved my job, I worked to adjust without complaint despite my problems with the male-dominated environment. My work was documented annually as required through written performance evaluations completed by my male supervisors and approved by the male chief probation officer. For nine consecutive years from 1975 through 1984, I received the highest rating of "excellent."

Between 1982 and 1984, I applied for three Supervising US Probation Officer promotions to supervisor. All positions were given to men less qualified than I.

In March 1984, I registered concerns with the Chief US Probation Officer and inquired why I was passed over for promotion. The chief provided no relevant or advisory response. Following that conversation, my life as a probation officer unraveled.

Paradoxically, male clients under my official supervision displayed more respect toward me than my male chief and supervisors in the federal court's own probation office. They subjected me to unprecedented criticism in every job aspect. My performance points were lowered despite expanded efforts to move closer to perfection since I was under hyper-scrutiny. Do you know or can you imagine the gut-wrenching impact of daily hyper-scrutiny?

However, I was not giving up on advancement. When a new position for promotion as a Chemical Dependency Specialist was announced in April 1984, I was the sole applicant and had the unmatched qualification of certification as a drug/alcohol counselor. Somehow, for reasons I could not discover — the position was never filled. Being passed over for promotion to a position for which I was uniquely qualified and had no competition convinced me to research outside options to address the cycle of promotion discrimination toward me. Would you have acted sooner? Remember (if you are old enough) that this was 1984.

Just before my 34th birthday in October 1984, I visited the Equal Employment Opportunity Commission (EEOC) for information and learned their authority did not extend to me, a federal court employee. Following EEOC advice, I contacted the probation office clerical supervisor who provided copies of the 1980 Judicial Equal Employment Program (JEEP) for federal court employees (which had not yet been used) and the Recommended Guidelines for Adverse Personnel Actions in the US Courts (REGAPA) available to file complaints. The clerical supervisor had obtained the copies…from-my-supervisor.

After requesting information for filing adverse action complaints, every bit hit the spinning blade. By chance, I discovered my supervisor was adding adverse notes in my personnel file without required notice to me. Next, I was eligible for a pay raise on November 1, 1984; but, one day before, I was handed a <u>second</u> "annual" evaluation—against policy. No one else received one. My supervisor downgraded my 9-year record of excellent performance ratings enough points to "very good" status, which disqualified me to receive my pay raise.

Aware of the precedent set by the chief probation officer when he raised a male officer's evaluation 70 points, I registered my objection to my unfair rating with the chief. He refused to budge my score. <u>I was not awarded the raise I earned.</u> The chief's inaction was the terminal straw on the shoulders of my efforts to break down inequity and mistreatment in the probation office. After researching, I retained an experienced discrimination lawyer. I saw no better chance for solution. Would you have?

My lawyer filed my sex discrimination complaint in US Magistrate Court on January 4, 1985, under the JEEP and REGAPA procedures. I felt relieved to have a dedicated legal advocate, and yet fearful of the (unknown) worst ahead.

The initial "shocker" was the named defendants (the chief probation officer and supervisors) were provided FREE legal counsel by the US Attorney's office because they were "court employees." I was a "court employee" in the same office, too. Can you figure why the defendants were given free representation and I was not? I knew it was unfair, but recourse was unavailable. The defendants were represented by the US Attorney's office, full of lawyers who filed multiple motions to limit or compel "discovery" and "stays." The delays ran me dry on funds and depleted my energy while increasing my distress.

The pinnacle stressor was the US Probation Office Chief and Supervising Officers, named as defendants, and the US Magistrate Court, assigned as trial court to hear my complaint, were <u>part of the same</u> USDC/EDMO system. And the Chief Judge of the USDC/EDMO system was ultimately an unnamed "co-defendant" because the Chief Probation Officer (a named defendant) reported to the Chief Judge as his "superior." Because I was an "unwelcome" employee in the same district court system, do you think there could be cause for concern for a conflict of interest?

Adverse actions toward me escalated radically, which necessitated three more separate filings of retaliation added to the original complaint and added to my legal expenses, of course, but not the defendants. Finally, in July 1985 I was scheduled for my day in court before the US Magistrate Judge for a consolidated hearing. My lawyer and I were well-prepared. However, prior to that date, the Chief Judge (the "unnamed co-defendant") issued an indefinite stay order blocking further proceedings on my complaint. My lawyer pursued legal remedies to lift the stay order and have my complaint heard. I could not fathom this happening. Can you?

Life continued. On January 24, 1986, I delivered our third child and began accrued leave (as I had for our two older children, then 5 and 6). While on leave in March, an unscheduled performance evaluation dated 9/10/85 to 3/3/86 arrived in my home mail. I was out of the office nearly eight weeks, yet my performance points were lowered.

But my supervisor did not stop there. He gave me one "unsatisfactory" mark on "Professional Demeanor and Approach to Job"—which was not a category involving "actual" work. (Do you think he meant "professional demeanor" as in —"get up on the table," sharing porn magazines, kicking holes in office walls, verbal harassment, bra plucking and snapping in the halls?)

The supervisor chose the "unsatisfactory" to re-classify my overall rating down to "fair," while my point score remained within the "very good" range. This "unsatisfactory" designation required me to subject to remedial actions upon return to the job I loved.

Anxiety rapidly raged and fear engulfed me, soul and body. I stood shaking on a precipice of indecision. My husband, a government worker, continued his support. How could I return to a hostile work environment? How could we afford the income loss with three kids? But the chief probation officer and supervisors had escalated attacks while I was absent-on-leave. What would you have done?

With a deep sense of loss and mental welfare necessity, I resigned as a United States Probation Officer on June 2, 1986.

Next, I filed for state unemployment compensation. Following an investigation, appeal, and formal hearing (with adversarial witnesses testifying), the Division of Employment Security-Appeals Tribunal granted me unemployment benefits in October 1987 based on their finding: "the treatment, including unjustified downgrading of the claimant…and a continued pattern of unfair supervisory behavior was a matter that would have compelled the reasonably prudent person similarly situated to forgo this employment…" (constructive discharge).

I might have felt a small victory, except my legal bills mounted due to new motions to have my complaint heard. Eventually, after a court appearance, a final order was rendered by the US Magistrate on January 3, 1989—four years after I filed. The ruling was unfavorable and vaguely addressed my basic complaint, much less the three retaliation filings. Scraping together money for new legal expenses, my attorney filed an appeal in the 8th Circuit, US Court of Appeals on January 9, 1989.

Sadly, my attorney unexpectedly passed away shortly thereafter. What now? Drop my appeal? Pay a new attorney? Go *pro se*? Your choice would have been …?

I represented myself before the federal appeals court, opposed by two US Attorney's Office lawyers defending the probation office defendants. The appeals panel of four federal judges verbally admired the way I presented my case, professionalism, and "lawyerly" skills.

In 1991 (two years before Ruth Bader Ginsburg joined the US Supreme Court), the US Appeals Court ruled on my suit—filed seven years earlier. The judges found compelling evidence of retaliation and ruled the defendants guilty on all three counts of retaliation and awarded me…(Can you guess?)…a total of under $2, 000 with zero reimbursement as the prevailing party for my giant legal expenses. The Court ordered the General Accounting Office to pay me. Sparing you the details of collection attempts, I never received a penny.

The guilty defendants suffered no known negative consequences, which stung me worse than walking into an enormous swarming beehive with eyes wide open. But I admit, I was far more incensed and incredulous! How could this be?

While the road I travelled pales in significance to that of Justice Ginsburg, our challenging paths were similarly in the legal/justice system. We shared the 70s/90s time frame. I imagine the injustices Justice Ginsburg endured (silently or not) on her path to becoming a US Supreme Court Judge!

The 80s were a time of high-profile national sex discrimination cases in the news from both ends of the spectrum. Mine was covered twice in our paper. In 1988, Time Magazine reported on an accomplished female manager in an investment company. Male colleagues branded her "macho" and "harsh," told her to wear make-up, and go to charm school. Her advancement was blocked. A female assistant state attorney in Florida who wore fashionable feminine attire to court was told she looked like a "bimbo." After complaining to the EEOC, she was fired.

In June 1988, the *Washington Post* reported on a female attorney (my age) in a federal agency who found her male-dominated environment was like a "brothel." After complaining of sexual harassment, she became a target for serious retaliation. Ultimately, she won her case but paid a high price.

As a pioneer female federal probation officer, I found that my: assertiveness was judged as abrasiveness; initiative was insubordination; review of constructive feedback was refusal to accept criticism; effort to collaborate indicated failure to accept authority; application for promotion demonstrated an expectation for undeserved advancement; and complaint of discrimination showed hostility. These factors of gender inequality and sex discrimination were expressed from the male chief and supervisors who stamped me as being "unprofessional" and "unqualified" for promotion. Has this happened to you or someone you know?

I am often asked whether I would do it again. Translated version: Would I spend seven years, pay legal expenses greater than $30,000 (1980s dollars), be forced to quit a job I loved, suffer tremendous mistreatment, spend thousands of hours preparing, suffer self-esteem hits, endure pressure, stress, embarrassment, and lose income—simply to receive the validating judgment from four honorable men of "YES, they surely did retaliate against you"…?

My request is for you to answer first for yourself, please—would you do it again? My answer comes later.

Going in, win or lose, I wanted to know whether it was OK for anyone to be treated like I was. Naively, I expected to have an answer after a few months and a few thousand dollars in one of two ways: either needed corrections would be implemented, and I could stay, or I would depart that toxic environment because unfair treatment was condoned. The situation twisted differently.

My answer to the translated version of the question, which is <u>informed</u> by what I now know is he## NO!...But I had no crystal ball. It is not a "real" question…impossible to answer. I cannot "un-know" the results and then answer the question now. Here is the best I can do—after 30 years.

My recent research for writing this story re-ignited latent pangs of emotional distress that overwhelmed me decades ago. But those emotions were overshadowed by my realization of the invaluable life lessons I chose to learn—lessons not available elsewhere. <u>Pursuit</u> of justice is a painful but righteous goal in itself despite personal outcome. Inevitable reverberations trigger future positive changes beyond the self.

Personal benefits bypassed me but are inherited directly and generally by women—several of whom are my daughters, nieces, and granddaughters. And unknown numbers of people, including our sons, benefitted from my efforts. (While my case was pending, the probation office hired more women and promoted one to supervisor while transparently attempting to use that manipulation in court to refute the sex discrimination charges. The court did not buy it.)

Attempting to disregard influence from the past outcome, I can say YES, I would do it over again to create the change that helps others—and possibly me.

On the subject of creating change, Ruth Bader Ginsburg said, "… If you want to be a true professional, you will do something outside of yourself … Something that makes life a little better for people less fortunate [or *less able* (my words)] than you." My battles against sex discrimination were painful yet injected me with wisdom and changed the lives of others.

After sharing intimate highlights and lowlights in my life, perhaps I can trash those piles of discrimination documents I saved for 39 years and dumped into the hefty banker boxes—overflowing with multi-colored, fat ring binders, transcripts, manilla files, and loose paper…or maybe not.

Was I—destined to champion women's equality? What would you vote I do with all that evidence and "stuff"?

*Def. "impudent": not showing due respect for another person: impertinent: insolent.

Dr. Patt Pickett, SEICC, LMFT, MEd, PhD, known as The Marriage Whisperer®, is a Licensed Marriage/Family Therapist and certified emotional intelligence coach. For over 30 years, since resignation as a US probation officer, she offers therapy, coaching, consulting, educational services, and online assessments. She co-owns St. Louis Emotional Intelligence-HireCoach™, a mental health/wellness practice. Emotional intelligence, marriage/relationships, family, and communication are her specialties. Dr. Patt completed teacher licensure, emotional Intelligence coach certification, and Level 2 of the Gottman couple's method.

Her latest book, *"Keep Strong Together: Relationship Quotes for Adult Coloring and Couples' Workbook,"* is part of her Relationship Keeper Series, a collection including easy-read relationship books and card decks. Appearances include Facebook Live as "WiseAce360" and TV/radio/workshops.

Dr. Patt is known for expressing her "outside-the-box thinking" which prompts many to announce, "I never thought about it that way before."

She and her husband enjoy their couple time. They have 5 children and 9 grandkids.

To contact Dr. Pickett and for more information about her services and the Relationship Keeper Series of wellness resources—self-help books, coloring books, workbooks, cards, and podcasts/webinars—check out www.PattPickett.com or she will be glad to hear directly from you by e-mail at DrPatt@PattPickett.com

ISABELLA BROWN

Growing Up After Ginsburg

Ruth Bader Ginsburg served in US courts and as a Supreme Court Justice long before I was born. I am nineteen years old, so her influence started before I was conceptualized, before my parents married, even before they met. I have never known a world that hasn't been touched by Justice Ginsburg, and my life would be nothing like it is today without her help.

I was raised by go-getters, both self-employed and both dedicated to fostering my confidence. If I had to describe my mother in one word, it would be "fierce." She goes for what she wants and won't stop until she gets it, tackling problems head-on and finding creative solutions without fail. I can always count on her to back me up, encourage me, and—put most simply—remind me to never take shit from anyone. And yes, she used those words way before I was allowed to use curse words. We don't take shit from anybody in my household. My father supported me similarly, although differently in execution. Endlessly protective and proud, my dad built my armor against the world with intellect. His many lectures, which droned on to my younger self, made me into who I am today. He reminded me that I am capable of achieving anything I want; that any low expectations should only fuel my fire; that I can prove the world wrong by giving others no choice but to pay attention; that I can outsmart and impress. My parents raised a determined, ambitious, confident, and capable woman. In RBG's world, I can more easily use these traits to make the world do my bidding.

However, if I'm being honest, I first learned about Ruth Bader Ginsburg in grade school at some point and could vaguely recognize her name if tested on it. In fact, seeing the sexism that still exists in this world was a relatively recent occurrence for me. As a girl, learning about the lack of rights women had in history felt like a distant experience. The idea of needing approval from your husband to perform basic financial tasks seemed a fantasy novel. In other words, I lived in blissful ignorance for a long time. When I sat down to write this chapter, I knew I needed to highlight that fact because I believe it's one of the greatest gifts Ruth Bader Ginsburg gave us. She has allowed young women like me, and so many girls in the future, to enter a world where inequality is not the first thing we see in our households. Instead, we learn strength and confidence early, then have the tools to tackle the remaining sexism head-on.

As I became more interested in the topic of gender, I learned more about Justice Ginsburg. And although her death has left a gaping hole in our forces against inequality, I don't want to focus on that. Rather, I'd like to share two lessons Justice Ginsburg has taught the world and I hold close to my heart. I say that she "taught" the world these lessons because she didn't just say them—she *lived* them and proved their efficacy. She did the hard work and showed us all what can be achieved. I hope that her example will lead more young women to grow to fill her shoes and, as they outgrow them, even help to further equality.

First, I believe that Ruth Bader Ginsburg was a perfect example of what my father lectured me about for so many years: She gave the world no choice but to listen to her. When Ginsburg was a student, she was recommended to Supreme Court Justice Felix Frankfurter when he needed a law clerk. He rejected her solely based on her gender. As we all know, Justice Ginsburg went on to fight for her beliefs and make a difference for years until, eventually, she became a Supreme Court Justice herself. This delicious irony demonstrates beautifully that Ginsburg was unrelenting in her goals and never let rejection stall her—especially rejection based on something so insignificant as gender. Instead, she kept working and showing the world what she could do. Often, she achieved even more than she was going for and then continued on.

There have been moments in my life where I've been discouraged by rejection, big and small. An example of one of the "bigger" rejections in my life was when I didn't receive the solo in a high school band performance I had worked very hard for. A "smaller" example was when I worked on a precalculus assignment with my three desk mates, all boys, and my solutions and suggestions were ignored by all three. The loudest of all of them even talked over my ideas.

After both of these experiences, following in Ginsburg's steps, I kept working and proving myself until I rose above the cynics and captured their attention. I gave everything I had to the band for a year after that heavy blow until I became the lead drum major, guiding the members of the band through our performances. As for the precalculus boys who ignored me? They found out after that day that my test score was just as high as theirs and started to pay me a bit more attention. Then, the boy who talked over me quickly found that I had a lot of interesting and important things to say—in math, in literature, and in quite a few other areas.

The second lesson I've learned from Justice Ginsburg became fairly popular after her death—and for good reason, considering the state of the United States during the 2020 election season. The relationship between Ruth Bader Ginsburg and Antonin Scalia is extremely interesting because it was such a positive one. These two Supreme Court Justices, who were opposites in so many obvious ways, from appearance to political views, were the best of friends. Their families even came together for New Year's Eve! Despite their differences and clear opposition to each other's views in the court, Ginsburg and Scalia found friendship in each other. Although they dissented so often on ideas in their work, they respected the other's views and welcomed debate and criticism. Ginsburg, although she completely disagreed with most of what Scalia said, remarked on how eloquently he spoke his ideas. And Scalia thought Ginsburg was completely wrong, but often helped her edit and strengthen her presentations.

To state the obvious, 2020 was exceptionally difficult for so many people and for many different reasons. One of the prominent problems I struggled with was the existential dread that crept in as conflict between people caused by political differences worsened. It seemed I could never escape hatred, anger, or disrespect for long; I saw it in public, in the news, and especially on social media. I witnessed more resentment between people in 2020 than any other year before, and I found hardly any resolutions to it. I myself have fought with loved ones about multiple topics this year. The riots in the Capitol in January of 2021 gave me an even more sinking feeling. It's all left me wondering how we can move past these conflicts and come back together.

I would never claim to know all the right answers on how America can move past this. I do know, however, that if Ruth Bader Ginsburg were alive, she would continue doing what she had been doing for so many years. She would be serving our country and welcoming debate at every turn. The example Ginsburg and Scalia set was the example we should all be following as we try to pick up the pieces of our country and the model we should think of in conflicts to come. Democracy requires debate. Democracy requires discussion. Justice Ginsburg's legacy reminds us, among other things, that no matter our differences, there is always room to uphold democracy.

There are so many more things RBG taught us through her incredible life, some of which I am sure you will get a sense of throughout this book. I feel that these two parts of her legacy are extremely powerful in today's world, though. Never giving up—in the face of rejection or in the face of seemingly impossible differences—is exactly what Americans need to do as we find our way again, together.

Isabella Brown is currently an undergraduate student at Northwestern University double-majoring in biology and creative writing. For the former, she plans to focus on genetics, then build a career in forensic biology. For the latter, she will focus on poetry and looks forward to composing throughout her life, with hopes to publish in the future. She is heavily involved in the Northwestern University Marching Band, where she plays trumpet, and is a staff manager and section leader.

Isabella lives in her hometown of Edwardsville, Illinois, with her mother and sister. She will soon reside in Evanston, Illinois, while she continues her studies.

Creative Writing Website: igbwrites.com
www.linkedin.com/in/isabella-g-brown

KARI MCGINNESS

Zedek, zedek, tirdof

Supreme Court Justice Ruth Bader Ginsburg instilled in me, in my almost half century of life, an extensive list of almost indescribable influences and inspirations. I feel goosebumps all over my body as I attempt to do her justice with words.

Like many women all over the world and this great nation of ours, I feel an immense amount of gratitude and indebtedness for all Justice Ginsburg has done for our rights and freedoms, despite our anatomical makeup, sexual orientation, physical challenges, or skin color. Because of this beautiful soul of a woman, Justice Ginsburg, having a vagina creates no legal blockades or dismissiveness. I believe we, as a society, need to follower her lead, to continue her fight for equality for all. Now on to my personal tRuth…

I grew up as a product of a second marriage for my mother. Before me, at the age of seventeen, she gave birth to my brother with her first husband. During that time, my mother worked two jobs to pave the way of success for him. This was during a time when women weren't encouraged to attain the same level of success as men. Women's careers and professional triumphs weren't celebrated to the degree they are today; in fact, they were often nonexistent. It wasn't until years later, after they divorced and she was left with no formal education or promising career opportunities, she decided her life would no longer be about advancing someone else's life; it would be about making my brother's and her own life top priorities above anyone else's. Wow, what a woman!

Fast forward years later and a second marriage to a man who encouraged her to be anything and everything she wanted to be. Along their journey together, a baby girl made her presence—Me. As a young girl, my parents told me I could do and be anything my heart desired, without resistance or hesitation. As a young girl I looked up to women like Frida Kahlo, Gloria Steinem, and Ruth Bader Ginsburg, my personal hero. My mother instilled this ideal in me and conditioned me to believe I could do anything my heart desired. As my mother told me, I now tell you: You can be the person you want to be. Being a woman gives you no less power or opportunity than anyone else.

When President Clinton appointed Justice Ginsburg in 1993, I watched it on TV with my mother. She said to me, "Greatness is about to be bestowed upon us. This woman will change the lives for so many, including us." And that, Ruth Bader Ginsburg did.

My mother went on to accomplish great things and inspired me each and every single day of my life. When she married my dad, she went on to work and gain that sense of independence she had lacked and longed for, for so long. My father's encouragement, the admiration she had for Justice Ginsburg and for all the female pioneers I listed above, motivated her. Because of the lessons learned from these powerful women and the struggles in her younger years, my mother taught me to be financially independent, to never rely on anyone other than myself, to dive deep into my convictions and beliefs without wavering from them, and to always remember I am my own woman.

In my youth, my mother became very ill with PVD (peripheral vascular disease). As a result, she was in and out of hospitals for most of my life. She lost both of her legs, twelve years apart, and acquired various ailments as a result of this ongoing illness. Losing her full independence was the hardest thing she endured throughout all her misfortunes. In spite of her illness, though, she continued to take care of herself. She was proud of that. I remember her once saying to me, "Kari, you should never NEED a man. You can WANT a man, but never NEED one." Despite her sufferings, she maintained what independence she could. She refused to let go of that. She would say, "Please, let me do things myself. I want to feel like a normal woman/human."

My father, who was the most loving husband and father I knew, never left her side for a second. He stood by her and encouraged her self-sufficiency and gumption. She refused to let the loss of her limbs and the deterioration of her body stop her from accomplishing what she wanted in life. She traveled and enjoyed life to its fullest, never letting her condition prevent her from being the woman she always wanted to be. She worked until she could no longer do so.

In my early twenties, I became faced with the decision no young lady wants to encounter but fears will happen to her. I was single, dating, enjoying my younger years. I became pregnant. There I was, a twenty-something-year-old woman, unwed, pregnant with a child I didn't feel I could care for. I was petrified. How on earth was I going to support myself and a child? I remember talking to my parents about my dilemma. Going into the discussion, I knew I would be faced with an abundance of support—without judgment. I was, indeed.

I will never forget the drive to the clinic to "handle" the matter. I cried the entire drive and most of the trip remains a blur to this day. As we pulled into the clinic, I remember people throwing things at our car, yelling, "Baby killer!" and "You're going to hell for this!" I remember being distraught hearing strangers yell these awful things at me, without even knowing me or my situation. I couldn't understand the judgment, I suppose. My father covered me with a jacket and escorted me into the building, shielding me from making eye contact with the protesters. I will never forget the feeling of his arms blocking me from all the hate. Hours later, upon leaving the clinic, I laid down in the car, sheer exhaustion radiating through my entire body, drifting in and out of sleep.

I struggled for weeks, years, and even to this day with the decision I made. Was it right? Was it wrong? One thing stands true: No matter my own internal conflicting thoughts or feelings, I was able to make that choice. I was able to make that choice because a female's choice matters. As Justice Ginsburg stated:

The decision, whether or not to bear a child, is central to a woman's life, to her well-being and dignity. It is a decision she must make for herself. When government controls that decision for her, she is being treated as less than a fully adult human responsible for her own choices.[1]

Even today, while I battle with my decision, I take comfort in knowing it was MINE. All mine. For that, I'm thankful. My body, my choice, my decision.

Here I am now, middle-aged, gray streaks peeking out from the crown of my head, crow's feet and inevitable wrinkles making their appearance alongside my

---

1 Olivia B. Waxman, "Ruth Bader Ginsburg Wishes This Case Had Legalized Abortion Instead of Roe v. Wade, Time, (Aug 2, 2018), accessed June 9, 2021, (https://time.com/5354490/ruth-bader-ginsburg-roe-v-wade/)

eyes (reflective of days and times gone by). I look back on all the things in my life that have been afforded me because of soldier women like Justice Ginsburg. Because of them, I am able to own and operate a successful business and be a woman at the same time. Thank you for affording me that opportunity, Justice Ginsburg. I can use my voice without fear of persecution. Thank you for giving me that gift, Justice Ginsburg. The level of equality amongst Americans you've created is life-changing for me and so many others. "Thank you" isn't enough; no words are. I believe, wholeheartedly, Ruth Bader Ginsburg paved the way for females to have a voice in their own lives and in the rights and freedoms deserved by everyone.

For my mother and people much like her, individuals inflicted with disabilities, Justice Ginsburg fought hard. Unfortunately, my mother succumbed to the disease in 2001 at the age of fifty-four. Whenever I start to feel weak, afraid, or frightened, I remember her strength and the strength she acquired from Justice Ginsburg. The resilience she maintained remains with me to this very day. It is what inspires me to be the woman I am.

As I sit here typing this, with a glass of sparkling wine in hand, I look back at how much my life has been (and will continue to be) impacted and influenced by RBG. I (we) still have a long journey ahead of me (us). I look forward to being able to cultivate my own destiny with my own hands and my own heart, without persecution or resistance. Thank you, Justice Ginsburg for being such a warrior queen and heroine for so many. Myself included.

(The title of this chapter translates to "Justice, justice, shall you pursue," and is a sign RBG had hanging in her chambers.)

Kari McGinness is forty-six years young, self-employed, fiercely independent, a free-thinker, and proud of her views and opinions. Women in her life helped her rid herself of the fear of honestly voicing who she is and what she believes. In her early adult years, Kari kept quiet about her beliefs and feelings for fear of upsetting someone or the reaction she might receive from someone holding opposing viewpoints. As she matured with age, mentally and emotionally, she learned others' opinions of her matter nil.

When given the opportunity to contribute to this book, Kari cried tears of joy and still pinches herself to remind her that she was given the chance to write about the one lady who inspired her as much as her very own mother. Kari says she is one lucky woman.

Thank you, RBG, for the courage. Thank you, Madam Justice, for the strength you've projected on to so many.

karimcginness@gmail.com
www.facebook.com/clevelandheath
www.instagram.com/karimcginness/
www.clevelandheath.com/
618-307-4830

HEIDI L. MARTIN

RBG, NLB, and HLM

As a financial professional, I've experienced both joy and frustration working with a diverse group of people. Putting complex financial puzzles together into cohesive plans requires knowing not only a person's finances but also their goals, dreams, fears, desires, habits, and relationship with money. In the financial community, this is known as "behavioral finance." The Corporate Finance Institute describes behavioral finance as the study of the behavior of investors. It focuses on the fact that investors are not always rational, have limits to their self-control, and are influenced by their own biases based on their history, experiences, cultural conditioning, and upbringing. My mother's life experiences in these very ways influenced and contributed to her behavior and decisions about money while she lived through the struggle of equality for women. She also influenced my beliefs. This chapter is dedicated to my mother, who in the spirit of RBG, I will refer to as "NLB."

I did not realize until much later in life what profound affects both RBG's and NLB's lives had on me, both personally and professionally. My mother, NLB, was born in 1929, the year of the stock market crash and subsequent Great Depression. NLB's grandmother ran a boarding house after her husband passed away; her mother was widowed and ran several restaurants, some of which she owned. Having had both a mother and grandmother who had lost their husbands at early ages, NLB was certainly aware of the need for household income and life insurance, though none of this was discussed with us when we were growing up. Instead, we were often told we could not afford things, so much so that one of my sisters said she thought we grew up poor. I don't agree as we never went without a meal, always had a roof over our heads, were clothed, given opportunities to participate in sports and music and to go places and do things that some of our friends never were.

NLB and my father, EAB, were married at a young age. They had nine children. At some point, both my parents purchased life insurance, though Dad's coverage was four times the amount of Mom's, a common and unfortunate practice in the financial industry for years. My dad was a hardworking man who worked for McDonnell Douglas as a machinist for thirty-five years and farmed in the evenings. Mom cared for us at home. NLB enrolled in nursing school after the birth of my youngest sibling in 1969. NLB amazed me. She had nine children and then decided to go to school so she could continue supporting us in the event something happened to Dad. Later, Dad developed health issues.

In the late nineteenth-century, a French anthropologist named Paul Broca made the claim that the volume of the brain determined intelligence and, since women's brains are smaller, they must be less intelligent. For years afterward, and likely even before, it was a common male viewpoint that women were delicate and couldn't understand things that men did. As a mother of three myself, you'll never convince me that my mother, who raised nine children, was delicate—and I don't have evidence that my father thought so either. My mother was a constant reader and intelligent. Women regularly faced discrimination in education prior to the late 1960s and into the 1970s; often they had to have permission to attend college or obtain a job. Though I never knew her to be an activist, NLB certainly benefitted from the work of RBG and the six landmark gender equality cases she argued before the Supreme Court while serving as the director for the Women's Rights Project at the ACLU.

Later, as I discussed financial matters with my parents, my mother would tell me to talk to Dad about it. NLB enjoyed being taken care of, and EAB certainly did that, even in financial matters. I wonder if Mom deferred to Dad because of conditioning from the laws she lived through or if she was merely disinterested in financial matters. Either way, I included her in our discussions, informing her of the importance of knowing what they had financially and what they did not.

In a 2009 interview with *USA Today*, RBG said, "Women belong in all places where decisions are being made. It shouldn't be that women are the exception." I believe that was true for NLB and it's certainly true for me, HLM, and all women.

Today, I often hear from clients that they should know more about finances, and I take the approach of educating my clients on financial matters. However, I believe that lack of financial education in our school systems, discriminatory laws, and law changes every few years leave people ill-equipped to handle basic everyday financial matters. The statistics of the lack of retirement readiness bear this out.

Growing up in the 1960s and 1970s, we heard a lot about the women's liberation movement. At the time, it seemed odd to me that my mother's name on my parents' bank accounts was not NLB, but Mrs. EAB. I thought how old-fashioned my mom must be to have her name listed on their checks and bank accounts that way. Little did I know at the time that the laws discriminated against women on the basis of gender, and it wasn't until the 1960s that women could open bank accounts in their own names. In fact, before the passage of the Equal Credit Opportunity Act in 1974, banks only granted credit cards to married women with their husband's signatures. Unmarried women were refused credit cards. RBG's work while an attorney with the ACLU paved the way for the passage of the Equal Credit Opportunity Act. Sometime later in my parents' lives, my mother's name was listed as "NLB"; though when they made that change, I am certain it was a direct result of the changes in the law. The idea that a woman could earn a living but not have credit in their own names financially hindered widows and divorcées.

Four years after the Equal Credit Opportunity Act was passed, the US Congress passed an amendment to the sex discrimination section of the Civil Rights Act of 1964. The Pregnancy Discrimination Act, passed in 1978, made it illegal to fire a woman for being pregnant. My parents had had their last child in 1969, but roadblocks for women before the Pregnancy Act was passed may have been a reason my mother did not work outside the home.

My interest in money and its functions began in my teens when I started my first job as a waitress. Suddenly, I was collecting tips each day and had a new sense of freedom. After having heard "We can't afford that" for so many years, I could buy my own clothes, buy my own record albums, and go to as many concerts as I wanted. I could afford it. Several mentors in my life encouraged me along the way. And like my parents, I worked hard at everything I pursued.

Finance interested me; and because of RBG's work at the ACLU and on the Supreme Court, I was able to pursue a career while pregnant, open a bank account in my name, buy property, obtain a mortgage, and obtain my own credit cards. I became president of a credit union in a conservative county. After several years in that position, I received a bonus for meeting all my goals set by the board of directors—I was terminated two weeks later because of my sexual orientation. Embarrassed, humiliated, angry, and depressed, I cried for days. How could they do this to someone who had worked so hard for them? It couldn't be legal, could it? It was.

Today, LGBT employment discrimination in the United States is illegal under Title VII of the Civil Rights Act of 1964, under the prohibition of employment discrimination, on the basis of sex. RBG wrote a majority opinion about this case in the 2020 decision.

Even though it may not have been her intention, RBG expanded the concept of gender discrimination, cleared the way for landmark LGBTQ decisions, and was a key vote in the decision to grant same-sex marriages. She opposed discrimination on the basis of gender and fought on behalf of both men and women, arguing that prohibiting protections based on sexual orientation violates the Fourteenth Amendment's Equal Protection Clause. In 2015, same-sex marriage became legal in all fifty states. My partner and I were married on our tenth anniversary together, made possible because of the groundwork of RBG and others. What a joyous day for us.

My termination eventually led to my career as a financial advisor and my focus on women and the LGBTQ community. Today, my financial practice consists primarily of women and LGBTQ clients who benefit from the work of RBG, as NLB and HLM have. Ginsburg was a tireless defender of justice, but there is more to do to bring this country closer to it's promise of equality for all. If I learned anything from RBG, it was to fight and overcome those who choose to suppress us. Let's get to work.

Heidi L. Martin, CFP®, RICP® has worked in financial services since 1981 and uses her experience to assist clients in putting together financial puzzles to meet their goals. Heidi enjoys working with women and members of the LGBTQ community in specialized areas, including retirement planning, investment planning, and risk management.

Heidi graduated with a BS in business administration from the University of Missouri–St. Louis with emphases in finance and marketing. She holds FINRA Series 6, 7, 63, and 65 securities registrations; is life, health- and long-term-care licensed; is a Certified Financial Planner® Practitioner and Retirement Income Certified Professional®; and is the secretary and Diversity Equity and Inclusion chair of the Greater St. Louis Chapter of the Financial Planning Association board.

Heidi enjoys an active outdoor life, diversity and education, and spending quality time with family and friends. She also likes traveling, swimming, cooking, and supporting and advocating for seniors, women, and the LGBTQ community.

www.heidilmartin.com
www.linkedin.com/in/heidimartin/
www.facebook.com/heidi.brakensiekmartin/

ALICE PRINCE

Always Last in Line

Justice Ginsburg was a woman of faith, a Jewish woman who unapologetically spoke up for minorities, the underserved, and disenfranchised communities. She integrated her faith in her work. As it has been said, you could tell her faith by her fruit. As a Jewish woman, Ginsburg believed strongly in justice for all—not just for persecuted Jews, those who looked like her, but also for the forgotten, the underserved and marginalized. For those who did not look like her, for those who needed it the most. For those persecuted, like the Jews, for generations. She climbed with all people and lifted them as she rose to heights in the legal and judicial arenas. She did not wait to invite them to join her at the crest of her success.

One could see her strong, courageous spirit through her daily walk through life. She authentically stood in the gap between acceptable and unacceptable, between discrimination and equality. She did this not for power or fame, not to bolster her career. She did it because it was the right thing to do. RBG rose to the occasion for not just women's rights but for the rights of all people who had been left behind or left out of the American dream. RBG followed this path; she made sure to help others from all cultures, all pathways in life, those persecuted like the Jewish. This is why people loved her. This is why I love her.

I am not a Jewish woman. I am a proud African-American catholic woman. And, like RBG, I believe in the importance of integrating my faith in every facet of my life. I believe in the importance of being a voice for the voiceless. I believe in standing in the gap for communities of color, communities of the marginalized and underserved, communities who have suffered for generations.

In this, my chapter, entitled "Always Last in Line," the communities I speak for are the communities RBG served throughout her career. The gap I speak of is the pandemic gap, the law-enforcement gap, the legal system gap, the education gap, the equity gap, the socioeconomic gap, the minority vs. majority gap, the man-to-woman gap. The always-last-in-line gap. RBG recognized that there are people in our community who are always, symbolically and physically, last in line. She worked endlessly to improve conditions for those last in line. Now, in the spirit of RBG, I say, *Huh-huh, honey, we're going to make you the **whole** line.* Her spirit for justice for all is the reason she was nicknamed the Notorious RBG after rapper Biggie Smalls, the Notorious B.I.G.

Like the Notorious B.I.G., RBG was unapologetic in her beliefs and her actions. Both blazed their own trails. Both lifted and climbed at the same time, bringing their people—not just the ones that looked like them, but all people— along with them. For example, growing up as a Jewish woman during the height of anti-semantic perspectives, RBG spoke out against the wrong, the injustices, loudly and proudly. Although life for the Jewish people was hard, she did not stop speaking up for justice. Speaking out was tough back in her day; I know it is still tough to speak out against injustices today. However, Justice Ginsburg paved the way for women like me to be a beacon of hope and a catalyst to the truth.

As an African-American woman, I grew up feeling the remnants of systematic racism, environmental racism, institutional racism, and the impact of economic racism. It is hard to undo and overcome the impact of over 400 years of bondage, historical lies, housing redlining, generational poverty, cultural defragmentation, employment discrimination, and food shortages. The 1987 mass shooting when two men walked into the only major grocery store in the area and claimed the lives of five supermarket employees shut the store down permanently, leaving only convenience stores or liquor stores for the community's "shopping convenience." The closing of the supermarket created community food deserts, meaning a shortage of healthful and affordable produce, like fresh vegetables, fruits, and meats. The food desert in turn deteriorated into a mudslide of assorted illnesses and health disparities, including obesity, diabetes, and hypertension. All maladies for which the African-American population is known and for which local quality healthcare and medical treatment is unavailable within their own communities.

My own grandmother moved from Baltimore, Maryland, to St. Louis, Missouri, to earn her nursing education at Homer G. Phillips Hospital, the only hospital west of the Mississippi to train African-American nurses and doctors.

"Always last in line" is the symbolic and physical position of the African-American family. "Always last in line" refers to governmental policies, such as moving minorities into low-income housing. Federal housing projects drove African-Americans, single mothers, into high-rises and urban areas to reduce monthly rent. However, the policy stated fathers could not live in the homes or the family would lose the apartment. The 2017 book, *Behind the Fog*, by Lisa Martino-Taylor, documents the US Army's experiment on residents of St. Louis's eleven-story Pruitt-Igoe project that subjected them, without their knowledge or consent, to harmful substances. It is unthinkable that the government put something in the ventilators for the women and children to inhale in the name of their experiment.

One thing I admired about RBG—she did not care about being labeled an angry woman. She was angry about the injustices she saw. Unlike RBG, I do not want to be construed or depicted as an angry black woman. But it is still a reality for African-American women who speak up for justice. In spite of that potential perception, I stand in my belief. I stand in the name of justice and equality. I stand in the shadow of RBG.

"Always last in line" is my way to remember from which my ancestors and past generations rose from the ashes to realize their American dream. I genuinely believe I and other women like me are our ancestors' wildest dreams because we are standing on the shoulders of great women like Justice Ginsburg. We will not settle. We will not be last in line. We will not allow other women to be last in line. We will speak up and speak out about injustices. We will work to change policies to prevent discriminatory practices such as redlining. We will work to be innovative through technology. We will run for offices and sit on city councils to restore and populate food deserts and to open avenues to quality healthcare services.

For me, "always last in line" means we stop thinking only that we deserve a seat at the table. We *must believe* that we deserve to have more than just a seat at the table. We must start thinking, *Do I actually want a seat at that table? Maybe I want to build a new table. Maybe I want to design and supply the materials for the* table. Or maybe I want to curate the space for the table. We must believe we can take our seats and sit anywhere we want. We will no longer be last in line. Having your feet up on the table doesn't mean you deserve authority. Women will sit, feet on the floor, and be the authority.

Justice Ginsburg has a rich history and a long legacy. She had a cult-like following because she believed in the power of empowering others. RBG believed in the importance of lifting and climbing at the same time, together, not just when she got to the mountaintop would she bring the people up. She'd take them with her on the journey. Like me, she realized the true treasure is found in the journey.

In my daily life, I will lift and climb. As I move to new professional and personal heights in life, I will always bring others along with me. I will not settle for being last in line and I will teach others how not to settle. Living through the legacy of Justice Ginsburg, I will always empower the future generation. As the Notorious B.I.G. passed the mic to RBG who passed the mic to the next generation, I pass the mic to you.

Alice M. Prince, Ed.D., is a native of St. Louis, Missouri, and graduate of St. Louis University, where she received her bachelor of science degree. She went on to Webster University in St. Louis, where she obtained a master of arts in communication management with an emphasis on crisis communication and a doctorate in educational leadership.

The recipient of multiple awards, including Economic Empowerment, Excellence in Workforce Development, Community Trailblazer, Phenomenal Woman Award, Women Who Inspire, and Phenomenal Women in Leadership, Dr. Prince serves on the board of directors for Catholic Charities, is a member of Delta Sigma Theta Sorority Incorporated, host and executive director of the *Good Morning Saint Louis* television show, and the CEO and president of Pathways United.

Dr. Prince is married to Carlton Prince, has three children, two dogs, and one granddog. She is a notable children's author and loves to play the harp. She released a single on iTunes, "Issa Vibe."

Website: dr-alice-prince.com
www.linkedin.com/in/draliceprince

CARIN FAHR SHULUSKY

Swimming Up Stream

In May of 1969, a young woman at the University of Missouri saw a flyer outside one of her agricultural classes encouraging all graduating seniors to attend a job fair. The flyer promised interviews for new grads from the School of Agriculture with leading agricultural companies. The opportunity that interested her most involved selling agricultural products to farmers and farm stores. Bright and eager for a new challenge, she grabbed one of the flyers.

On the specified day, she donned her best Sunday dress, put her hair in a neat bun, added a conservative amount of makeup, and marched to the interviews. Full of nerves and excitement, she opened the door and walked in. In front of her, a row of men in suits, the kind her father had worn to church, sat on one side of a long table. A fellow classmate had just finished his interview; she thought it would be her turn next. The man on the far right looked at her puzzled.

"What are you doing in here?"

"I've come for the job interview you're advertising in this flyer. I graduate from the School of Agriculture in two weeks. I'm from a farm family, and I'd love the chance to work for you"

"But you're a woman," the first man declared, rather loudly.

Very observant, she thought. "Yes. There's nothing on this flyer that says, 'Men only.'"

"Well, we don't hire women," the tallest man answered. "This is a sales job. You'd have to travel from farm to farm. A woman couldn't do that. Besides, most girls go to college for their 'Mrs.' degree anyway. You're a pretty girl. I'm sure you'll have one of those soon enough. Men need to support a family."

"I'm not married. I don't plan on getting married anytime soon. I grew up on a farm. Both of my grandparents were farmers. I can do this job."

"Doesn't matter," said the man on the end. "We don't hire women."

The interview was over. She held her temper, her tears, and left the room.

This young lady's story—my sister's story—was repeated all across the country in 1969. There weren't "glass ceilings" then, rather steel doors, shut soundly to women. But I always knew I was destined for bigger things.

When I graduated from college in 1973, the government was pressuring companies to hire women—perhaps due to Ruth Bader Ginsburg, who had changed the climate for women from 1969 to 1973 by arguing over 300 cases of gender discrimination for the ACLU. In 1973, a major US conglomerate invited me to interview for a job. They offered me the position, and I became the first professional woman in that division. Certain I was at the top of my game, I had confidence enough to fill a moving van. But that's pretty much all I had.

At twenty-two, I took my few possessions and left St. Louis for the Berkshire Mountains. When I started the position, I was about as naïve as a young farm girl could be. But after two years there, nothing much could surprise me. I worked hard and did an admirable job for a new college grad. But nobody—I mean nobody—wanted me there. The secretaries (the only other women in the place) thought I had slept with someone to get that job. I ate lunch alone. The men (I learned later) thought they'd be accused (by their wives) of having an affair with me if they asked me to lunch.

Once, I attended a meeting where a salesman presented opportunities to advertise in his publication. I walked into the room and he turned bright red—all-out Christmas red.

"I can't give my slide presentation with her in the room."

My boss said, "She's part of the team. She stays."

The flustered salesman continued the presentation—during which I found out why he had turned red. In between slides of the merits of advertising in his publication, slides of naked women displayed on the screen. I tried my best to remain unmoved, but nothing in my education had prepared me for this. It repulsed me, but I couldn't show it.

After the presentation he said, "You should let people know you will be in these meetings." To which I replied, "You should change your presentation. There will be more of me."

In my job, I wrote and produced product sheets for the plastics division of the corporation. These sheets touted new applications for polycarbonate plastics. Details about the applications came from our sales team—all men, of course. One of the top salesmen was in town for meetings and had information I needed. After his meeting, I asked him to come by my office, which I shared with Fred, the nicest, least offensive man in the company. Our conversation went something like this.

Me: "Carl, I understand you sold polycarbonate plastic for a new application in Atlanta. Can you tell me about it?"

Carl: "I could tell you a lot of things if you'd have drinks with me."

Me: "I don't want drinks, Carl. I want the information I need for the product sheet. I think the application is a blender, right?"

Carl: "You do look very cute when you're trying to be all business. I know we could have a good time together. How about we take off now. We can always do this stuff later."

Me: "I have no intention of having drinks or anything else, Carl, but I would like some information from you. What is the name of your client? Did you work with a molder or the end user?"

Carl: "How does a cute little girl like you know those kinds of words? There are so many other words I'd like to discuss with you."

At this point, dear old Fred was rolling out of his chair laughing. I didn't think it was in the least funny. I knew I was never going to get the information I needed to do my job. I left and went to the ladies' room, where Carl couldn't follow. I sat on the toilet and cried for twenty minutes. If only I had known about Ruth Bader Ginsburg back then... There was no one to listen.

If Carl was horrid, my bosses were worse. My main boss, Mark, got a promotion to Schenectady, New York. The whole office, minus secretaries, took him out for drinks. Harmless, right? Of course, I was the only woman, but I was getting used to that and I kept my head high. Mark thought I had been doing a bang-up job. He seemed to be my defender.

It was a good party. I danced with Fred and a few others I trusted. Mark asked me to dance. While we were dancing, he complimented my work and said he wanted to take me along to his new position. It would be a big promotion but I deserved it. That made perfect sense to me. I *did* deserve a promotion. And I welcomed any change from the constant sexual harassment. No place could be worse, right? Then Mark started breathing into my ear. He said when we finished here, I should show him my apartment. We would be a good pair. I thanked him and said I needed the ladies' room. I found a back door and ran to my car.

Once home, I cried until I fell asleep. Not because the boss I had admired turned out to be a misogynist creep, but because I knew at that moment that I was not the brilliant young marketing genius I thought I was. I knew, too, I wasn't ever the prettiest woman in the room either. I knew what they wanted from me, and it wasn't my talent or good looks.

Mark gave me two gifts: First, he demolished my over-confident, arrogant self. I never again overrated my talents. Second, he taught me caution: to always assume the worst and be pleased when I am wrong. I wasn't wrong all that much.

A few months later, I was called upon to help the marketing team develop a major presentation for the national sales meeting being held in a resort in Puerto Rico. In January, I was thrilled to be escaping the bitter cold of Massachusetts for the Caribbean. We had worked long, hard hours on the presentation; we had meshed into a team. Two days before our scheduled departure for Puerto Rico, the general manager came to my office and said I couldn't go on the trip. My boss protested, "This is a huge effort. Carin's been a major factor in developing the presentation. We need her there."

"You don't understand. There will be 300 men away from their wives, drinking and partying. If she goes, she'll get raped. We can't have that. It wouldn't look good. If you need her in Puerto Rico, she can stay in San Juan and send her work to our resort via cab." With that he left.

"But why would he say something like that?" I asked Fred. "Surely, he has better control over his sales staff than that?"

"No, I don't think he does," Fred answered. "Actually, two years ago, a tourist was raped in our hotel during one of our national sales meetings. I think it was him."

"Why wasn't he arrested?"

"She settled for a fortune."

I went to San Juan and stayed away from the drunken rapist sales team. I worked hard, sending about three cabs a day to the resort. I expect I had more fun reading on the beach and sipping a cocktail—one, only one—than the team had. From that time, I developed a plan for all business meetings that I practiced throughout my career: When out of town, I had one cocktail and dinner with my co-workers, then I retreated to my room and locked the door. Later, I discovered the men had gone to a brothel. I also discovered that my co-workers often obtained prostitutes for clients. But at least they had the good taste to never discuss it.

On one trip to a plastics convention in Chicago, the marketing team had planned to entertain prospective buyers over dinner at the best restaurants there. I made all the arrangements and represented the advertising team at the convention. While at the 95th-floor restaurant of the John Hancock building, I had trouble explaining our marketing strategy to a prospective client. It was my conversation with Carl all over again. I gave up and went to my out-of-town strategy: one cocktail, dinner, and room—alone. The client, the next morning, apologized for acting so strange. He explained that he thought I was the "entertainment" for the evening. Stunned, I couldn't respond.

In 1975, a recession devasted the company. I can't say I cried any tears over that, but I did lose my job. Fortunately, I found a good job with the agricultural division of a large Midwest corporation and became the first professional woman in their corporate office. Some of the men I worked with welcomed me—it may have helped that I was married by then. I worked hard and received awards: four Archie awards for achievement in marketing and one National Agri-Marketing Association award. Yet I was passed over, again and again, for promotions. After five years and losing my dream job to a man three pay levels below me, whom I had trained, I had had enough. I filed a claim with the Equal Opportunity Commission. I won, but the solution was too little too late. By then I was a mother and holding my daughter was more important than continuing that fight.

I am proud to say that by the time I finished my career, I owned my own marketing company and hired women—some men, if they were good enough.

I've presented the tip of the iceberg here. But who knows where we would be without the brave Ruth Bader Ginsburg who continued the fight for women's rights right up to her last breath? Thank you RBG.

Carin Fahr Shulusky attended University of Missouri, Columbia, receiving a bachelor's degree in journalism. After college she worked in advertising for GE Plastics and Monsanto.

After twenty-five years in marketing, Carin created her own firm, Marketing Alliance. She served as president of the Business Marketing Association of St. Louis and received their Lifetime Achievement Award. Her professional and community organizations include the National Association of Press Women, Special Education Foundation, and Springboard.

Carin and her husband, Richard Shulusky, live in St. Louis and have two children: Christine Shulusky Blonn and Andrew Shulusky, and a granddaughter, Sophie Blonn.

Carin's first book, *In the Middle,* was inspired by her own battle to care for her beloved mother, Dorothy Hoehne Fahr.

Carin is a lifelong member of Pathfinder Church in Ellisville, Missouri, where she has taught Sunday School and VBS. She has served on short-term missions to Belize ten time.

carinshulusky.com
www.facebook.com/cshulusky
www.instagram.com/cshulusky/

DIANE FINNESTEAD

The Little Engine That Could

...But though it seemed that she could hardly pull herself along / She hitched on to the train and as she pulled she sang this song / I think I can, I think I can, I think I have a plan / And I can do 'most anything if I only think I can...[2]

You may be thinking, what in the world does "The Little Engine That Could" have to do with Justice Ginsburg? I was hoping you would ask.

In the late 1990s, eastern European immigrants, mainly from war-torn Bosnia, started to immigrate to the United States. The city of St. Louis, my home-town since age three, welcomed these immigrants with open arms. My mother was the assistant director of relocation for the St. Louis real estate firm, Coldwell Banker-Gundaker, in the late 1990s. Through interpreters, she worked with clients relocating from across the globe in their home-buying experience. During those years, tax abatements made relocating to the city of St. Louis appealing and affordable. Ethnic enclaves, often located within a particular St. Louis municipality, developed strong neighborhoods to support mutual success in business while celebrating common heritage through shared cultural and religious traditions. St. Louis Italians discovered this when they founded "The Hill"; then the Irish discovered the same when they settled in "Dog Town"; then the Polish when they entered north city; and the Germans and Dutch when they originally immigrated to south city/south county. Today, south city/south county includes the largest

---

2 Watty Piper, *The Little Engine That Could*, GP Putnam's Sons, (2001).

Bosnian population outside of Europe. Currently, there are 300,000 Bosnians in America and 70,000 in the St. Louis area[3], making this area centered around Bevo Mill known as "Little Bosnia."

The school year was 2003-2004. Recently divorced, I decided to leave the insurance industry, dust off my teaching credentials, and re-enter the field of education as an elementary music teacher for St. Louis Public Schools. My post was at a south city school where the student population was over eighty-seven percent Bosnian. All students were eager to become English-speaking naturalized Americans. This community actively embraced me—ultimately naming me "Ms. Musica." They also embraced our Fourteenth Amendment and the promise of life, liberty, and property. I expected my teachings would benefit their pursuits. What I didn't expect was the life-changing gift I would receive at the end of the year.

To meet the goal of teaching English through music curriculum, I had the flexibility and freedom to be creative, fun, interactive, and engaging. Thank goodness! With props, pictures, handheld manipulatives, puppets, costumes, instruments, drums, recorders, technology, and just about anything you can imagine, I brought lyrics to life and met the needs of every learner.

I think I can, I think I can, I think I have a plan / And I can do 'most anything if I only think I can...

One enthusiastic kindergartner loved everything I did. He mastered all my lessons, animations, mannerisms, and musical interpretations. He knew the core of the kindergarten music curriculum, demonstrating faster/slower tempo, louder/softer dynamics, higher/lower tone and timbre. Moving to the front of the class and speaking of himself in the third person, he'd announce, "The Magical, Fabulous Feriz would like to teach." And when the Magical, Fabulous Feriz would "teach," he would nail it every time; then look me in the eye, smile, and say, "How I do, Ms. Musica?"

"Ask me again," I'd say, "and this time ask, 'How did I do?'"

"That's what I ask." Then the whole class of twenty-five five-year-olds would laugh, clap, smile, and cheer "Brava! Let Magical, Fabulous Feriz do it again!"

"Take it away Feriz!" I'd say. And he'd do it again.

---

3 Amelia Flood, "Healing Words: SLUCare Staffers Bridge Communications Gap Between Patients, Physicians," Saint Louis University, (Mar 21, 2018), accessed on June 6, 2021, https://www.slu.edu/news/2018/march/bosnian-interpreter-bonds.php.

I had become accustomed to hearing his echoing feet in the corridor as he bounded down three stories of steps into my basement music room of our turn-of-the-nineteenth-century school. However, on the last day of the year, I was busy packing up for the summer when Feriz announced himself three times at the top of his voice.

"Here comes the Mighty, Magical, Fabulous Feriz to take you, Ms. Musica, to the yard!" With that, he ran into my room and grabbed me by the hand. "Come, come see. They speaka da English!" Excitement bursting, Feriz took me toward the schoolyard. Just before we got to the doors, he demanded I close my eyes. The doors opened. I felt the sun on my face.

He whispered—but not to me—"Are you ready?" Then he said, "Open your eyes now, Ms. Musica, and hear the English." Feriz—fashioned after me—began directing—"One, two, three, four." Eleven female Bosnian senior citizens stood before us, all wearing their hijabs, and in a sing-songy chorus, sang:

There was a little railroad train with loads and loads of toys / All starting out to find a home with little girls and boys / And as that little railroad train began to chug along / The little engine up in front was heard to sing this song…

They sang twenty-three other songs that Feriz had taught them from my classes. When the concert ended, amid applause, hugs, and praises for Feriz, tears of joy streamed down my face. The ladies' faces too.

"They all take their American citizenship test next month," Feriz said.

"How did you teach these ladies that song?"

"Because it's like the little engine," he said. "I think I can, I think I can…I knew I could, I knew I could." Maybe it is that simple to reach the mountaintop of outstanding achievement. To believe, *I think I can. I think I can.*

In 1963 the US had passed the first legislation guaranteeing equal pay for equal work, yet the career categories this applied to were not made clear until 1972 when salespeople, executives, and administrators were included. The definition and interpretation continue to evolve today. In October 1974, President Gerald Ford signed into law the Federal Consumer Credit Act, which stated that a woman could own her own home without a male cosigner. Prior to that year, all single, divorced, and widowed American women had to bring a man along to cosign. Even in 1996 when buying my first house as a single woman, on closing day, two male title company representatives asked me, "Who else is to be included on the title?" When I replied. "Just me," they both pressed, "No husband or father or brother you'd like to include?"

I was shocked but this had been a practice or inquiry from decades prior that had not been updated. Caught off guard, I felt as if the biggest purchase in my life wasn't as important as being a wife, daughter, or sister to a man. The cat got my tongue. Well, thank goodness my Realtor mother was at my side and picked up on the fact that I was momentarily stupefied. Without missing a beat, my mom gave these two gentlemen an authoritative look, pointed professionally to my preliminary paperwork, and stated matter-of-factly, "Just her on the title, thank you. It's her money. It's her house and her mortgage payment." I still wonder how many women had also gone through this antiquated, unnecessary type of Q&A when, as new homeowners, they should have felt over the moon—not judged! RBG has stated, "My mother told me to be a lady. And for her, that meant be your own person, be independent."[4] These were the same pearls of wisdom my mother shared with me as I was handed the keys to my home that day. "Now you decorate and celebrate!" my mother said. Justice Ginsburg believed in the importance of celebration too; in fact, the iconic justice is quoted on a t-shirt sold by redbubble. com, "There's a sense that time is precious and you should enjoy and thrive in what you're doing to the hilt."

So we celebrate. The Federal Consumer Credit Act made life better for millions of women who once could not be approved for credit without a man's signature. And thanks to the accomplishments of Justice Ginsburg and the Women's Business Ownership Act of 1988, women of all ethnicities can be approved for business loan without a male cosigner. Prior to this act, a seventeen-year-old son would have sufficed as cosigner for women business owners who had no husband, father, or brother. Additionally, Amnesty International expanded the definition of "rights" by saying, "Women's rights are human rights…These include the right to live free from violence and discrimination; to enjoy the highest attainable

---

4 Alexander Kacala, "20 inspiring and empowering quotes from the late Ruth Bader Ginsburg," Today, (Sep 18, 2020), accessed on June 4, 2021, https://www.today.com/news/ruth-bader-ginsburg-quotes-20-inspiring-ideas-rbg-t192057.

standard of physical and mental health: to be educated; to own property; to vote; and to earn an equal wage."[5]

By the time, the Bosnian community arrived in America in the late 1990s, gender equality in the US had already made giant steps forward. RBG, and women like her, had influenced change around the world so that the Bosnian women and others who immigrated to the US were free to seek an education, better jobs and careers, credit, and business ownership—free to pursue a better life in the US. No longer would they be subjected to discrimination based on their gender.

Before me on that last day of school, I sensed enjoyment and celebration, while, under the direction of five-year-old Feriz, the Bosnian senior ladies sang their self-fulfilling prophecy, *I think I can, I think I can*. After that schoolyard gift, Feriz's title became "The Miraculous, Mighty, Magical, Fabulous Feriz," and the following month, all eleven ladies became American citizens. Under the recent changes in US laws, some also went on to become homeowners and business owners—owning bakeries, restaurants, maid services, automotive and tailor shops, et cetera.

I marvel and celebrate all people who give of themselves to forward the lives of others, like Feriz and RBG. I reflect on the life of tiny, yet mighty, Notorious RBG. I imagine she could identify with the spirit of Feriz and that little engine too. She soared in her career despite challenges and setbacks as she passionately strove to help all of us become better Americans because *she knew she could, she knew she could*. And to pay tribute to RBG, let all of us continue to make positive, contributions to continue her work and to affirm: *I think I can. I think I can*.

There is still more work to do. But how will we know when we have made a difference in equal rights for women? How will we know when we have climbed to the pinnacle of RBG's goals? RBG's response to Gwen Ifill in February 2015 on the *PBS NewsHour* may explain: "People ask me sometimes… When will there be enough women on the court? And my answer is when there are nine."

The phenomenal leadership of RBG continues even after her death. And we must carry on. Sometimes it takes a long time for the little engine to climb the mountain but, in the words of RBG, "Fight for the thing that you care about but

---

5 "Women's rights are human rights!"Amnesty International, (n/d), accessed June 4, 2021, https://www.amnesty.org/en/what-we-do/discrimination/womens-rights/.

do it in a way that will lead others to join you,"[6] we can make it up that mountain. Let's hope Justice Ginsburg's tenacity, *I think we can,* becomes our *I knew we could.*

---

6 Alanna Vagianos, "Ruth Bader Ginsburg Tells Young Women: 'Fight for the Things You care About,'" Harvard Radcliffe Institute, (June 2, 2015), accessed June 4, 2021, https://www.radcliffe.harvard.edu/news-and-ideas/ruth-bader-ginsburg-tells-young-women-fight-for-the-things-you-care-about.

Diane is thrilled to be a contributor to this anthology in tribute to Justice Ginsburg. From insurance to music teacher to elementary principal, Diane Ruth Finnestead returned to insurance in 2014. Recognized as a leading producer in life and health insurance nationwide for those under age sixty-five and those who are Medicare-eligible, Diane advocates health reform through National Association of Health Underwriters and serves on the St. Louis board, recruiting industry professionals who share the same passion for providing intelligent insurance options to their clients.

Diane credits her ability to help thousands of Americans over the past twenty years to find the right insurance due to her background and career in education. She holds a bachelor's degree in music from the University of North Texas, a master's degree in teaching, and a second master's degree as an education specialist from Webster University. She also completed post-graduate work at the University of Memphis and Northwestern University.

314-302-5743
Diane Finnestead You Tube
www.dianeinsurancestl.com
www.LinkedIn.com/in/diane-finnestead-mat-Ed-s-4187912a/
www.Facebook.com/dianeinsurancestl

Remember the Gentlemen

"Why don't you become a nurse or a teacher so you will have something to fall back on?" That was the advice I received from my parents as a young person contemplating my future after high school. The point being, "to fall back on" meant my occupational ambitions were expected to be temporary, just until I had a husband to support me and I took my proper role as a homemaker and then mother. I deeply resented that advice. My internal dialogue said, "*Are those the only options you see for me?*" Not to denigrate nurses or teachers, both noble occupations, but I didn't want to be segregated into a "female occupation." Unless you came of age in the 1960s, it is hard to imagine the level of occupational segregation by gender that existed in the United States. Not only did the help-wanted ads list jobs **in print** by female and male occupations, but the gender socialization such as I experienced with my parents' comments was quite common. In high school, girls took home economics and boys took shop. Girls were told they were not good at math and science. It was an interesting time to come of age.

Ruth Bader Ginsburg broke the gender inequality mold by graduating law school in 1959, a point in time when this was extremely rare. Viewing the biopic film, *On the Basis of Sex*, about her early life, I was struck by the scene showing 500 white male youth going into Harvard Law School on opening day and the eight odd women sprinkled in the freshman class auditorium. This is a stark reminder of what it was like in the sixties before a whole generation of women fought for gender equality. Now, it is taken for granted that women can enter any occupation for which they show ability and desire.

When I has a young girl, I read a book about Nellie Bly, a nineteenth century investigative reporter that so inspired me I wanted to be a journalist. Bly had such an exciting life. She did undercover work and traveled around the world. What an example she was to me of the possibilities in my life.

In my current job with a Chamber of Commerce, I was just finishing up a board meeting when one of the board members came up to me and remarked, "We need to have gender balance on the board." The suggestion took me aback. At the time, we had a board comprised of eight females and seven males, and we were contemplating new board member candidates. Some of the proposed persons mentioned were female; and this board member, who I highly respected, was concerned that it was getting "too female." I had not thought about gender balance and was only thinking of good people that could enhance our organization—an organization that was founded in 1937 as the "Businessmen's Association." We can imagine how diverse that association must have been in 1937! My board member's comment had me thinking that men begin to get uncomfortable with "too much" representation of women in decision-making roles. It also had me pondering the status of equal representation in our elected offices, something I have worked for as part of the National Women's Political Caucus of St. Louis.

The representation of women in our legislative bodies is growing at a snail's pace. In Missouri, where I live, the state legislature is just 26.4 percent female. In Congress, female representation grew from 20 percent to 26.5 percent in recent years. Only in Nevada has the state legislature passed the milestone of becoming a majority female legislative body with 60.3 percent women. I wonder, is that making the males in that assembly uncomfortable and asking for "gender balance"?

Ruth Bader Ginsburg once was asked, "When will there be enough women on the Supreme Court?" She famously replied, "When there are nine." I must admit, her answer made me pause. Then she went on, "For most of our history they have all been male and no one said a word." Since all-male judicial and legislative bodies have so recently been the norm, it appears jarring to conceive of the reverse.

"Remember the ladies," wrote Abigail Adams in 1776 to her husband, John Adams, and members of the Continental Congress while they were drafting the first United States Constitution. John Adams ignored his wife's suggestion, and gender is not mentioned in the Constitution. American women in the eighteenth and nineteenth centuries had a decidedly inferior status in legal standing, professions, education, and more. The 1920 victory giving women the right to vote was the first amendment to begin encoding legal gender equality.

It was only in the latter half of the twentieth century that many gender norms began to be dismantled in earnest. Ruth Bader Ginsburg was a giant figure in dismantling this history. Ironically, she began by "remembering the gentlemen" to invoke an analogy from Abigail Adams. Ginsburg began dismantling gender discrimination by defending a man for inequities in the law. Her first case was in 1970, *Moritz v. Commissioner*. A single man, Charles Moritz was denied a tax deduction for hiring a nurse for his ailing mother because he was not "a woman, a widower or divorcée, or a husband whose wife is incapacitated or institutionalized." Ginsburg won her case and found her confidence as a lawyer. She went on to argue numerous cases before the Supreme Court, many times having male plaintiffs. She argued that gender inequality negatively impacts all genders, something we still experience today.

Like many women, I have tokens of RBG's influence sprinkled in my house. A couple of magnets with salient quotes reside on my refrigerator, a dangling wooden ornament of RBG hangs from my reading light in the library room. At Christmas-time, I have an RBG ornament of her likeness. I recently received three RBG-labeled wines as a gift. The local independent bookstore has a whole section of RBG books and trinkets. She has become a merchandise- marketing phenomenon that could rival any Disney princess aisles in a retailer's toy section. It is laudable that a woman in her eighties could become this amazing meme and pop icon, beloved by generations of women and men who believe in gender equality.

Having just finished my bachelor's degree in women and gender studies, studying something that really wasn't even available to me when I was in my twenties, and after more than fifty years of being a college dropout, I have become aware of how important gender socialization is and how we unconsciously don't see this phenomenon. The overwhelming lesson of my studies is that gender is a social construct. In the famous words of feminist Simone de Beauvoir, "One is not born a woman, but becomes one." We are socialized into female expectations in the same way men are socialized into certain stereotypes of masculinity. Gender studies matter.

One of the beautiful things about Ruth Bader Ginsburg was her relationship with her husband, Marty Ginsburg, who shared equally in child-rearing and championed her career. She may not have made it to the Supreme Court without his advocacy. He put forward her nomination in front of the media and women's rights organizations and was instrumental in her acquiring the nomination. He is my role model for a husband in a society that equally values both genders.

We have come so far, and Ruth Bader Ginsburg has led the way in knocking down so many of the legal obstacles to gender equality. She demonstrated that through perseverance, inner strength, and having a team we can make change, one step at a time. We would do well to listen to the message her life represents and follow the trail she blazed.

Rebecca is a communicator through her writing, podcasts, storytelling, and events. She claims affinity to all three waves of feminism, often joking that she "breathes is three centuries." She reenacts nineteenth century feminist philosopher Elizabeth Cady Stanton. She came of age in the twentieth century during the Women's Liberation movement. Now in the **twenty-first century**, Rebecca works to advance gender equality with renewed passion. Along with her reenactment of Elizabeth Cady Stanton, Rebecca has been joined by Sojourner Truth and Susan B. Anthony reenactors, and they perform as a trio of monumental women of the nineteenth century.

Rebecca has a BA in women and gender studies and is a Distinguished Toastmaster award recipient. She is a Chamber of Commerce executive in St. Louis County and produces a weekly podcast, "What's UP Around Town."

As a member of the National Women's Political Caucus, she is currently involved in writing the history of the founding mothers of the St. Louis caucus.

314-800-4050
rebeccanow@sbcglobal.net
www.rebeccanowandthen.com

JL GRAY

Fairy-Tales and Backpacks

The omniscient mist sparkles as it meets the faded jade oak leaves encompassing the entire horizon. Every few steps, the upturned roots of a fallen giant oak tree showcase yet another entire ecosystem of insects, plants, and more. Unexpected sightings of moss coverings and fungi flowering with random and delicate orange and pink petals add to the allure and entrancement of hiking the Georgian Appalachian Trail. Fairy-tale-like promises of fairy-tale adventures, with the promise of even more magic at every "next turn."

The glamour of all these spellbinding delights camouflages the realities of the drudgery, tenacity, and resolve to actually travel the Appalachian Trail. The glamourous magic, actually, can seem more sorcery than magic up close.

This is the tale of RBG and me spending six days in the Georgia mountains backpacking together, talking about life, and coming to only tentative conclusions.

Ruth and I were not always friends. As most people know, Ruth's contributions to the world at large were quiet in the making, monumental in the effects. For me, I did not know too much about her, despite having just finished law school a few years before she was appointed to the US Supreme Court. In law school of course, I had memorized all the current members of the court, and I knew whether each justice leaned liberal or conservative, having just studied the most important current Supreme Court cases. Once law school was complete, though, I was immersed in the practical sides of law (Where's the file? The client is on the phone! Will the judge yell at me if I use blue ink for my signature instead of black?—et cetera, et cetera.) All I seemed to be aware of was that Ruth Bader Ginsburg was yet another moderate on a panel that was increasingly moving away from the left. Once RBG became a meme and then as we all watched her get sicker and eventually die, I, like many others, became reacquainted with Justice Ginsburg and her legacy.

So when I was walking the Appalachian Trail earlier this year, I was thinking about this, and how I had always seemed to view the Appalachian Mountains as "moderate mountains." Usually, I said Appalachian "mountains" with air quotes: I had grown up in Colorado and spent my early years and many of my best life-moments in the Rockies. THOSE were mountains. But the Appalachians…yeah, pretty, sure…but you know…moderate. How complex could this be?

Before we had become reacquainted, Ruth Bader Ginsburg seemed to me to just be so moderate in so many ways: a small woman with a tiny voice; she was no force-of-life Martin Luther King! She seemed…admirable, really, really smart, but *moderate.*

Then came the Lilly Ledbetter case, and President Obama's highlighting of those issues when he signed the Lilly Ledbetter Fair Pay Act. As a lifelong, amateur verbophile, I immediately, of course, was intrigued that this was called the "Fair" Pay Act rather than the "Equal" Pay Act. And of course, I loved the alliteration in Lilly Ledbetter's name…I was intrigued, and so for the first time in over twenty-five years, I actually read the Supreme Court opinion and the brilliant (and dare I say, sassy) dissent penned by Justice Ginsburg. The glittery, "shiny objects" in the name of the act itself, the alliteration of Lilly Ledbetter's name, and hearing Lilly Ledbetter, herself, speak drew me to the case; similarly, it took photos of the magically shimmering leaves of the Appalachian trees and the teeny tiny fauna, ferns, and fungi to draw me to the Appalachians. Teeny tiny leaves, teeny tiny plant life, and a teeny tiny Supreme Court Justice—all camouflage for what lay inside once you take a closer look.

So, starting down these paths—both the path of getting to know RBG and the "path" otherwise known as the Appalachian Trail—my expectations were surpassed by the realities in completely unexpected ways. From photographs, the Appalachian Trail appears so serene (and it is) and so soothing to the soul (and it is). But it also can be neither of those. The Appalachian Trail, in photographs, appears to be a slowly ascending and descending wooded path through beautiful wilderness…and it is. But once you are actually walking that path, you realize this is a journey of up and down and up and down and up and down…climbing over small boulders sometimes for miles at a time can be exhausting, even though the boulders are "small," and especially if you are a vertically-challenged woman with knees that have seen better days.

But I was thinking about RBG while walking. How she was so small and, of course, toward the end of her life, small, frail, and ailing. But RBG famously stayed with her planks, so I could soldier on over those boulders. After all, I had "hiked" for months in preparation; granted, I had not "backpacked," only hiked. How much harder could it be??

The unexperienced perspective rarely matches the experienced perspective. Ruth Bader Ginsburg didn't seem to have too hard of a life. Just read a lot of opinions, accumulate a life's worth of high-level intimacy with the legal issues of gender equity, and then apply those skills to the problems at hand. (At this point, I am sad that sarcasm is so difficult to project in writing. Please note that as an attorney, I hold the work of all judges in the highest of esteem.)

But Ruth Bader Ginsburg was not HIKING through the woods; Ruth Bader Ginsburg was BACKPACKING through the woods. Anyone who has hiked and then backpacked, carrying two to five pounds and a water bottle versus carrying twenty-five to fifty pounds of gear on your back every step of the way, knows that what you carry on your back affects every step, every hop, and every decision regarding how fast to go, how long to go, and when to stop. Hiking and backpacking may not look that different to the casual observer; similarly, being a trial lawyer and being a judge (and then a justice) may not look all that different, but they are.

Ruth Bader Ginsburg picked up the backpack of the burden of soldiering forward in the name of gender equity at the beginning of her trail, even before becoming a lawyer. As many people already know, RBG married before law school, had her first baby while in law school, and took care of her ailing husband during law school. Despite challenges that leave most people exhausted just thinking about them, RBG didn't just carry that backpack, she crossed the finish line first in her class at Cornell Law School in 1954. Before she could practice law, she had already embodied defiance of social norms. She "walked the talk" before she even said a word.

RBG's challenges in finding a job are well documented; even once she was a law professor at Rutgers, she had to file an Equal Pay Act complaint just to be paid the same as her male counterparts. In 1969, at the request of her students, she taught her first seminar on women and law and then founded the *Women's Rights Law Reporter*; and from there, her trajectory to becoming the eminent and most effective single influence on legal gender equity had begun. Later, as a Columbia law professor, she not only co-authored a book on sex discrimination but she also advocated for the female maids on staff at the law school when she learned the women janitors were laid off before the male janitors. In 1972, she co-founded the Women's Rights Project of the ACLU. She was fearless. She tirelessly climbed every boulder in her way, up and down, up and down.

And then there was Lilly Ledbetter and the 2007 dissent in the *Ledbetter v. Goodyear* case. Like untold thousands of other equity advocates, although sorely disappointed with the court's opinion, I was titillated with Justice Ginsburg's language and thrilled with President Obama's 2009 signing of the "Lilly Ledbetter Fair Pay Act," which addressed the statute of limitations barrier to many fair-pay complaints like Lilly Ledbetter had faced. It was at this moment that RBG and I became better acquainted. Justice Ginsburg explained to her peers in this dissent that the realities of how pay disparities can be "insidious discrimination" that build up "slowly but steadily," and thus the statute of limitations cannot be applied in the same way as it is applied to an easily identified act such as improper firing and illegal grounds for promotion. "Pay disparities often occur, as they did in Ledbetter's case, in small increments; cause to suspect that discrimination is taking place develops only over time." *Ledbetter v. Goodyear Tire & Rubber Co., Inc.* 550 US 618, 645 (2007). Justice Ginsburg was **schooling** her fellow justices on the "real world" truths about which some of them seemed to be ignorant. Justice Ginsburg became my real-world hero.

Justice Ginsburg's personal contributions toward gender equity were not just monumental; "Herculean" would be the better descriptor, as she was just one tiny person carrying much of the weight of the world. To those who do not look closely, her life may seem fairy-tale-like—like the Appalachian Trail—sparkly with pleasing, unexpected delights along the way. But the truth is that Justice Ginsburg backpacked relentlessly and tirelessly; she faced boulder after boulder, and no doubt that backpack felt impossibly heavy at times. Although not always successfully, she relentlessly challenged and attacked the status quo. In the wake of losing her, we have only tentative conclusions on how we as a society can go forward to make the law, and our world, a more equitable place. For me and so many others, RBG set the gold standard for how much one person can accomplish simply by staying the course and fearlessly "spelling it out" when those in power seem to be oblivious to the real inequities of the world. Just climb over those boulders, one at a time, and stop every once in a while to take in all the magic and beauty in the world.

JL Gray

Although an attorney and mediator by day, JL Gray is at her core a verbophile, with a lifelong array of experience, both writing and teaching writing. She has taught literature, expository and creative writing classes, and seminars at all levels, including high school, college, MBA, and other professional programs.

JL Gray has always instructed her students that the best way to improve their writing is to read, read, read. Having belonged to over six book clubs in the last fifteen years, JL Gray is practicing what she preaches. Her 2021 goal is to complete seventy-five books; her lifelong goal is to complete one book from or featuring every country in the world. It's good to have goals!

JL Gray has lived in the St. Louis area since 1988 with her husband, three sons, and a zoo's worth of animals. She enjoys reading, writing, teaching, and practicing law.

KRYSTAL WEIGL

The Dissenter's Hope

Justice Ruth Bader Ginsburg's contributions to society are nothing short of legendary. Justice Ginsburg's work in gender discrimination challenged and ultimately changed countless laws reinforcing discriminatory gender roles. Opinions she authored enhanced the protections of civil rights of minorities and our environment, and expanded the court's recognition of different legal schools of thought. Her accomplishments are featured in A-List films; she's one of the nation's most influential people and a pop-culture icon—all the more remarkable when you consider that she attained celebrity status with a career in the humdrum field of law. Her notoriety and iconic contributions to America has cemented her image in pop culture by branding her "The Notorious RBG," in homage to fellow Brooklyn icon Biggie Smalls.

You probably aren't reading this book to learn about Justice Ginsburg; you can do that through film, textbooks, court opinions, or even her autobiography. I'm not the right person to teach about the late justice or her works. In fact, you may be asking yourself why I've authored this chapter in the first place. Allow me to introduce myself. I am Krystal Weigl, an average lawyer who has an unrelenting passion for the perfection of a more just legal system. I'm someone who thinks the law should create a more fair and equitable society. Most importantly, I'm someone who thinks that it can. That's why I'm the right person to describe the ways Justice Ginsburg's work has fueled my own.

It's likely because of Justice Ginsburg's endless successes that I'm drawn to the events where it appears, at first glance, that she did not succeed. It is also, in part, because I have had my fair share of setbacks;

and inspiration to push through them is sometimes in short supply. Justice Ginsburg's struggles to find work, almost entirely due to sexism, resulted in her hand-selecting cases to further her goals. The justice was reportedly asked by the dean of Harvard Law why she was taking a man's spot in the class. She responded by finishing top of her class and writing for the *Harvard Law Review*. Her dissents were marked by bold statements in her personal collar selections and thoughtful optimism about the rationale she authored. The challenges Justice Ginsburg faced are often and easily overshadowed by the many wins she racked up along the way. This writer finds her wins to be more influential, inspirational, and noteworthy in light of her handling of more than her share of obstacles.

Her perseverance was partially thanks to her commitment to and belief in the power of the law. Specifically, the power of the law as a force for good. Justice Ginsburg couldn't have had the impact she had on civil rights, nor done the work she did, had she not considered this work critical. A lifetime of achievement, benefiting the underserved underdogs of the justice system simply doesn't come about without lifelong dedication to such a cause. It's fair to say she believed it was possible to change and better society through the law. This belief has fueled my legal career and my work as an attorney.

Once upon a time, Professor Bear's Preschool honored me with the "Star of the Week" award. The poster I made read: "Favorite color, purple; favorite animal, unicorn; dream job, lawyer." This was remarkable for several reasons: I barely knew what lawyers were, had a pretty minimal resume, and still had all my baby teeth. (Shout-out to my mom for writing it because I didn't know how to spell "lawyer.") Despite all that, I knew lawyers were well-dressed people who solved problems for other people. I also knew lawyers did this because they understood how the rules worked. In later years, I'd learn lawyers also knew how to work the rules. In the twenty years it took to go from pre-school Star of the Week to Juris Doctor, these truths pretty much held up. Lawyers are people who can help.

In 2017, Justice Ginsburg gave an audience at Stanford some insight into the power of the law. She spoke about the difference between having the skills to practice law and learning the ability to use it for good.

I tell the law students…if you are going to be a lawyer and just practice your profession, well, you have a skill…very much like a plumber. But if you want to be a true professional, you will do something outside yourself. Something to repair tears in your community. Something to make life a little better for people less fortunate than you[7].

I understood her to mean, go learn the skills you need to learn to help others.

During my time in the three-year escape room they call "law school," I regularly thought about why I was there. I also thought about whether I belonged there in the first place. (That's a reflection for a different day because I now know that I did.) When I agonized over my study habits, my skill level, my intelligence, I told myself I was there to learn how to help others. I learned quickly during my time in the inspiring offices of Hiscock Legal Aid that plenty of lawyers felt the same way. That meant, no matter what my contracts' grade was (and it was not great), I was on the right track.

My path through the law has been nothing short of wayward. I've worked in human rights and policy advocacy, medical malpractice and personal injury, pharmaceutical litigation, civil rights, intellectual property, small business law, and a tremendous amount of contract negotiation. (I'd like my professor to know that I'm quite skilled now at negotiating contracts!) My practice took me from Syracuse, New York, to Washington, DC, Chicago, Illinois, and back home to St. Louis, Missouri. Very little of this was planned. Each organization I joined I found a role where I was able to help. In small ways, big ways, and everything in between, learning to be a lawyer has helped me help others.

My career choices have left me asking more questions than a toddler at a dinosaur exhibit. I've moved firms so many times that sharing those numbers might make the LinkedIn talking heads explode. Spoiler alert: You don't have to wait two years every time you move firms. I've reinvented myself, my work, and my practice area so often I've lost count. The reason has been, each and every time, because I was called to help in an unexpected way. I moved back to my hometown when my family needed some support. This led me to land and ultimately resign from my dream job because it was a toxic workplace for me and

---

7 Kathleen J. Sullivan, "U.S. Supreme Court Justice Ruth Bader Ginsburg talks about a meaningful life," Stanford News (Feb 6, 2017), accessed June 3, 2021, https://news.stanford.edu/2017/02/06/supreme-court-associate-justice-ginsburg-talks-meaningful-life/

my female colleagues. I helped launch a technology platform to make law accessible to the everyday entrepreneur; that is, Legal GPS, which is now at many local libraries. I've represented domestic violence victims, without pay, because I knew the rules that could help.

These changes, challenges, and choices I've made have often left my head spinning. Moving jobs is hard. Learning things outside yourself is scary. Repairing tears in society feels both underwhelming and overwhelming most of the time. It's often as much as once a week that I wonder if I'm really cut out for it, if I'm the right person for the job, or if I've got it in me to calm one more client's panic attack. When this happens, I remember that, because I choose to help, I am the right person. I think about the many times I've worked outside my comfort zone to bring a solution to someone who needed one. I remember that knowing the rules, knowing how this game is played, and explaining it calmly actually lets clients move away from the panic so they can heal. I remember that tiny tears in society deserve repairing.

When people ask me what I do now, I often tell them, "I represent the injured and small business owners, and I help them with whatever it is they ask." That's the short version. My practice these days is mission-focused. It's not locked into a specific area of law. I help people make sense of contracts, file trademarks, invest in real estate, hire and fire employees, dissolve partnerships, avoid foreclosure, and more. I work with victims of discrimination and volunteer in community initiatives to create gender equality. And when duty calls, I represent the injured because I do it well. In short, I use the talent that I have and the skills I've learned as a lawyer to help my community. For me, there has never been a higher calling.

Justice Ginsburg's work was visionary. She was able to remain focused on the long game even when she sat atop the highest court in the land. Her writing was never so shortsighted or presumptuous to assume that her work was near completion. Her hope for the good work of the justice system transcended her own mortality. When she wasn't in the majority, meaning the court did not vote her way, she said, "Some of my favorite opinions are dissenting opinions. I will not live to see what becomes of them, but I remain hopeful."

There is no doubt she knew certain opinions and laws were wrong. She spent most of her life working to change the law. Her patience in change and hope for the future inspires me daily.

Dissents speak to a future age. It's not simply to say, "My colleagues are wrong and I would do it this way." But the greatest dissents do become court opinions and gradually over time their views become the dominant view. So that's the dissenter's hope: that they are writing not for today, but for tomorrow[8].

I'm no Supreme Court Justice, but I'm inspired by the dissenter's hope in the judicial system.

In true lawyer fashion, I need to add a short disclaimer. The law is not perfect. The justice system is immensely flawed. In too many ways to count, people are harmed by the disparate impact of justice, lack of access to the system, or laws deliberately designed to do harm. My writing is not a puff piece about how wonderfully our justice system works nor about how one woman changed the world. This piece is an acknowledgement that the law should, and most importantly *can*, work to protect everyone equally. It is a tribute to an idol who actively worked to change the legal system for the better. I'm learning my role in doing the same. The Notorious RBG's life and legacy inspires me to work through the blows that come with fighting the good fight.

I was riding in the passenger seat of my husband's car on a trip through Southern Missouri last fall. My brother texted asking if I'd heard the news. This kind of text is usually followed by bad news. I braced myself for an injured family member, a problem at the house, or something wrong in the neighborhood. Then I read, "RBG just died." My body reacted instantly, and I felt the tears begin to sting. I continued on my trip, noticing the ragged confederate flags, Trump paraphernalia, and closed businesses that littered the otherwise beautiful landscape of my home state. I, along with so many others, felt the enormous weight of her loss. The resolve I felt about continuing her work and continuing to "repair tears" in the community was surely not mine alone either. That is the power of her legacy: its enduring inspiration to keep fighting.

---

8 Message from Quinn McKew, "US: Justice Ruth Bader Ginsburg death of a champion of equal rights," *Article 19*, (Sep 21, 2020), https://www.article19.org/resources/justice-ruth-bader-ginsburg

I believe it will take me a lifetime to understand the justice's relentless faith in the power of the law. The law is supposed to protect. Lawyers are people who can help. These guiding principles came early and naturally to me. Justice Ginsburg's life and legacy has proven these truths. My practice will always be committed to stretching the law's protections to those it's designed to help. I, too, am committed to "using whatever talent I have to do [my] work to the very best of [my] ability."

Krystal Weigl is a practicing attorney, writer, and daydreamer. She is a proud alumnus of Illinois State University and Syracuse College of Law; she credits each school's mock trial programs for crafting her style of advocacy. Krystal has dedicated her career to making the law more accessible, approachable, and useful to those who need it. She's passionate about making the legal profession a healthier and better place for its professionals. The highest client praise she's received is that she's "a different type of lawyer."

Her time away from court is spent working on community initiatives to enhance equality and create opportunities where they're lacking. Krystal writes fiction novels about hopeful, strong-willed women; works on her soon-to-be-launched wellness initiative for lawyers; and attempts golf. After moves to Syracuse, Washington, DC, and Chicago, Krystal settled with her husband, Andy, in her hometown of St. Louis, Missouri. (Go Cards!)

LinkedIn: www.linkedin.com/in/krystal-weigl-916448210/
Facebook: www.facebook.com/krystal.weigl/
Twitter: @_Krystal_withaK
Instagram: krystalweigl

Agent of Change

Born on the Ides of March in 1933, Ruth Bader Ginsburg (RBG) became a pioneer and major influencer of the American legal/justice system and remained in that role until her death in September of 2020. Upon her passing, I reflected on and learned more of the great many contributions attributed to this dynamic woman and decided to discuss her life with the younger members of my family. When I asked my ten-year-old grandson, Judah, if he knew Ruth Bader Ginsburg, he said, "Well, Grammer (as he affectionately calls me), her name is familiar to me but I'm not really sure why. It seems to me she was famous and that she died last year. I believe she was on the Supreme Court."

Bursting with pride, I said, "Yes," as I thought to myself how wonderful he knows any current events in such a chaotic time of the pandemic and the resultant distance learning. But it was clear he knew no other facts about her, about what she had stood for; or of the crusading topics of her life. During my time of reflection, I decided I would like to teach my grandchildren more about how I saw this powerful woman, RBG.

My process of reflection took me back in time to compare the benchmarks of my own life as paralleled to the work of RBG. I was in junior high and high school during the 1960s, an era that we look back on to see hippies, bell bottom pants, sock hops, proms, and protests. Social consciousness was expanding in those years, and behind the scenes were brilliant people who were changing the laws that ruled the norms of the time. RBG was one of those champions of social justice.

Justice Ginsburg graduated law school in 1959 and became the first female editor of the *Harvard Law Review.* As a young married mother, she figured out ways to break through the front door at law firms and continue to press ever upwards breaking "the glass ceiling."

During that same time, I was growing in my own social awareness. It was a time in our public high school (yes, this was a public school!) to challenge the system and wear pants to class. Can you imagine a dress code allowing only skirts? This small rebellion may sound ridiculous, but girls were not allowed to wear pants to school back then, only skirts—and skirts had to be a certain length. Teachers and administrators judged skirts to be too short by having the girl get on her knees in front of them. The hemline had to measure two inches above the floor and no more. More than two inches and the girl would be sent home to change. And this was at a time when movies depicted the miniskirt, a trending fashion that took the hemlines to approximately eight inches above the floor. With authorities' rules such as these, inequities became more apparent to me. I wanted to be a "rule follower" and not "rock the boat," but...

Others were fighting on larger platforms. I became aware of laws—such as that, in certain states, women could not have credit on their own and that women weren't always able to own property. These things were changed from behind the scenes by the people who made the laws and interpreted the Constitution. People like Ruth Bader Ginsburg.

When I got married fifty years ago, I would never have dreamed of keeping my maiden name. It just wasn't done unless you were one of those California-liberal-hippie types. Luckily, I married a progressive man who questioned the social norms as much as I did. For my twentieth-fifth wedding anniversary, I took my maiden name back in a renewal of vows ceremony. I went from having my husband's name, "Licklider," back to my maiden name, "Powers." The change signified my transition to being a more progressive, powerful person, like those social icons I admired including, Ruth Bader Ginsburg and her willingness to fight for freedom, to fight for each of us to be individuals, to fight for our rights to be equal under the law. In all ways, always.

So just as I took you back to my high school days of not being able to wear pants to school, let me remind you that the sixties erupted with transformations in culture, via rebellions and protests for civil rights and injustices. Multi-racial families often found stares of strangers following them. Bi-racial couples did not appear on television, nor did interracial children. We had no examples on the screen of diversity or inclusivity depicting a marriage of a white man (or woman) and black woman (or man) and their interracial children.

Rights and injustices for gay and lesbian people, LGBTQ as we recognize them today, had not yet hit the cultural consciousness in the sixties. Society looked down on openly gay and lesbian people and considered the lifestyle shameful; it was the unspoken secret in the room. Legal same-sex marriages did not exist. Pride Parades did not happen. Shows like *The Modern Family,* a sitcom following the lives of three diverse families living in the Los Angeles area—one nuclear, one blended, and one same-sex (two Caucasian men who adopted a Vietnamese daughter together)—did not exist. RBG would become a resounding presence in the name of equality for same-sex marriages.

To live through the cultural shift and see in my lifetime the legislature and the legal system in the courts of our land (especially the US Supreme Court) find a way to bring recognition, legality, and equality for same-sex marriages to the law of the land in all fifty states was an absolute miracle.

When I speak to my granddaughter, Rozella, who is seventeen years old, she reminds me that she has the right to choose her pronoun. Although for her, the pronoun "she" is appropriate, many of her friends are gay, straight, or bisexual, and questioning their own presentation in the world. Things have changed in the world and culture of today. I support, honor, and applaud this transformation and self-identification. At the same time, I know that without people like Ruth Bader Ginsburg and her stand with the court for same-sex marriage it would not have happened in my lifetime. I have been an observer of the transformation in culture in the LBGTQ community. Ruth Bader Ginsburg also observed and she stood up for equality.

RBG listened to opposing views as she demonstrated in her lifetime friendship with Supreme Court Justice Antonin Scalia. Despite their ideological differences, they spanned the differences with a willingness to listen, understand, and respect each other and their differing points of view.

Lastly, in my reflections about how I'd like my grandchildren to remember such an important member of the highest court in our land, I thought of her powerful strength in overcoming obstacles. One of her first big obstacles was finding a job in the legal profession as a wife and mother. This woman overcame cancer three times, working through a full-time job in the public eye and in the high-stress environment of the Supreme Court.

Justice Ruth Bader Ginsburg died at the age of eighty-seven. She was still working.

Please think about this: RBG is a woman who went to work the morning after her husband of fifty-six years passed away. She took no days of grief and bereavement because she was in the middle of writing her dissent on a big case. It is the strength of overcoming obstacles that this small-in-stature woman demonstrated; but I would like to make note in my reflections, this is one of the reasons that she became "the notorious RBG"—quotation marks used there because she did it all in stride. She did it all with grace. And she did it all with perseverance and consistency as she held herself to the highest standards.

So as I reflect on Ginsburg and what I want my grandchildren to remember about this important woman in our history, I want them to remember that she was an agent of change. That the massive changes that were taking place in our culture were taking place partially because she continued to stand firm in her conviction that all men and women are created equal under the law and under the Constitution of the United States of America. It was equality that she fought for and it was equality for which she stood.

Rev. Pat Powers, an ordained minister with the Centers for Spiritual Living, facilitates workshops and weekend intensives, teaches classes, speaks to groups (both large and small), does personal coaching, performs weddings, is a fundraiser/auctioneer, has performed stand-up comedy, and sung the Blues for hundreds of conference attendees. Rev. Pat serves as a consultant and shepherds families through end-of-life conversations, leading to peaceful transitions. Celebrations of life and personalized memorials are her specialties.

Rev. Pat teaches a powerful, positive-thinking spiritual philosophy to the seekers of Truth, the "Cultural Creatives," who are looking for love, inspiration and fulfillment, and a way to leave the world a better place.

Rev. Pat lives in the St. Louis metro area. She has two grown children and three grandchildren. Bella, the Rottweiler, keeps close guard.

Life is good—All the Time!

To schedule a conversation just call or text 636-577-5000
www.facebook.com/revpatpowers
Revpatpowers@gmail.com
www.linkedin.com/in/pat-powers-0b58295/

CELESTE HARTWELL

Living in Divine Truth

Truth. We each have many truths that direct our lives. Sometimes it is truth with a lowercase "t," which Merriam Webster defines as "the real facts about something; the things that are true." Other times in our lives, it is Truth with an uppercase "T," and said to mean, by Merriam Webster, a transcendent fundamental or spiritual reality,"[9] as in Divine Truth.

Ruth Bader Ginsburg lived her life in the Truth of who she was on all levels. She pioneered for many women by breaking glass ceilings and shifting the paradigm of how women value themselves. She impacted male-dominated rooms throughout her career by being the only woman in many—she not only held her ground in those rooms but also set the example of how to be strong, fierce, and feminine all at the same time. RBG's model has not only inspired many different generations of women alive today, but I know her legacy will continue for future generations. We've yet to fully realize the influence she will have on the history of women in the workplace.

I relate to Justice Ginsburg. I am a woman who took a job out of high school at the local electric company, starting in a women-only clerical position as a remittance cashier, receiving checks in payment of customers' utility bills. I would then sort those payments manually, eventually running the payments through large machines that processed the payments and applied the money to the appropriate accounts. While in this position, I didn't work with or for men. Once I moved up the corporate ladder, though, I reached a place where I was the only woman in the

9 *Merriam-Webster.com Dictionary*, s.v. "truth," accessed June 8, 2021, https://www.merriam-webster.com/dictionary/truth.

room in many meetings and was one of a handful of women who were salaried in a municipal utility company. During this career, however, I deeply desired more. My Truth (capital "T") was that I knew I was here on this earth to help people on an individual level—not a faceless corporation.

My first desire for a vocation was to be a teacher, but I ended up at the utility company as it was the easiest job to land without education past a high school diploma. I continued my education as I worked in the electricity and natural gas industries, eventually attaining my degree in business acquisition and contract management—a far cry from the educational focus I had always envisioned myself doing.

I had some opportunities to train others throughout my nearly two-decade career in utilities, and I lapped up those opportunities like a thirsty dog on a hot July day. However, daily, I wasn't living in my Truth. While I had many smaller truths along the way, I wasn't living in the Truth of who I knew I was at my core: a teacher.

When I left corporate America in 2015, after some loud messages from the Universe that it was time to move on, I started following the breadcrumbs. Immediately upon giving my resignation, I learned that a career coach would be speaking at a local conference I had already planned to attend. Something deep in my soul woke up and nudged me to go and hear her. As she spoke about her journey and how she helped people, I was deeply moved and compelled to hire her. Throughout my work with her, I did deep soul-searching and learned that I desired to be a coach, speaker, and author. The discovery of the coaching and speaking industries would finally fulfill my lifelong desire to teach.

Next in my entrepreneurial journey, the question of who and how to coach was significant and one that, to find the answer, I had to move through many different truths. Over several years, following my inner guidance, I took steps even when I had no idea how they fit or where they would lead. At one point, I became a certified energy healer and even became an ordained minister, not always knowing why but following the deep sense of knowing in my body that these were my next steps. Finally, it all came together...

The beauty of this newly discovered purpose was that I could finally pour into my clients through coaching and speaking, whether through individual coaching, group programs, or masterminds (magical small groups of people brainstorming ideas on each person's business challenges or opportunities). It fulfills me, the same way training people in corporate had fulfilled me. The teaching that comes through in my work is natural and profound; it feeds my younger self's desire to be of service through education.

As I created podcasts, videos, and client lists, the formation of my business, Divine Feminine Leaders, was born. I say "born" because I believe that our businesses, projects, and ideas have a lifeforce of their own when we align with our purpose and passion. They wait for discovery; they tap us on the shoulder, introduce us to the people we need to meet, and take us by the hand to the places we need to go—but only when we're brave enough to follow. Divine Feminine Leaders does just that for me.

This is where the story profoundly ties into RBG. Through my work with women, I've realized women are still relatively new to the work environment. Generationally, women have been toddlers in the workforce outside the home, in putting a dollar value on their gifts, talents, and work. We're still new to knowing our value and standing firm in our worth. I often talk about this on the Divine Feminine Leaders Podcast because I absolutely know that when women know their value cognitively and feel worthy in their bodies, they show up more powerfully for themselves, their clients, and everyone who learns from them.

The other part of this that ties to RBG is that when women make money—amounts of money they didn't even know were possible when they were in their familiar family paradigms and generational patterning—*think $20,000 per month or more*—they not only take care of themselves but also take care of their families and their communities. When women make "abnormal" amounts of money, it is when they're able to do what one of my favorite coaches termed "Putting their money where their hearts are."

When we, as women, are financially independent of others, we don't suffer through relationships for fear of losing safety and security. When we trust the Universe or our Higher Power to take care of us, we know that our safety and security comes from within; then, and only then, are we able to show up, enact profound change for the people we love and care about, and allow that to ripple out through our communities and eventually the world. When women realize *they* create their lives in every way, when women heal their relationship with money, and when women wake up to their worthiness, they have healthier, more loving relationships in all areas of their lives. They become magnets for all they desire.

This is Justice Ginsburg's legacy: Ruth Bader Ginsburg loved herself so deeply she knew her worth, knew her value, and also knew she could do anything she desired to do. Because RBG accepted her Truth, she not only took care of herself first, but she took care of her family, her community, and eventually enacted profound change in the highest court of the United States— as a woman first and also as a Supreme Court Justice. She was a woman of vision, a woman living in her Truth, and a force of nature.

How can you live your life more similarly to RBG today? What qualities would you like to embody? If you desire help with healing or coaching, I invite you to reach out, and I look forward to helping you step more fully into living your Divine Truth.

After an eighteen-year career in corporate, Celeste Hartwell jumped off the ledge of safety and security into the unknown of entrepreneurship. She first fell into listening to well-intentioned people who guided her against her internal knowing of her own business. Then she learned to tune into her own internal guidance and created a business and life she adores.

Passionate about helping women, Celeste works with women to cultivate a relationship with their own intuition so they feel excited and energized about living a life without compromise and helps clients heal their relationship with money. Through the work of her company, Divine Feminine Leaders, women step out of overwhelm, guilt, and shame, to shine brightly, attracting all they desire.

Celeste hosts three podcasts: Divine Feminine Leaders, Divine Silence, and The Ease of Business. Join her on Create More Courage and Confidence—a free five-day experience at http://bit.ly/createmoreconfidence.

Listen to her Podcasts here: www.divinefeminineleaders.com/podcasts/
Connect on Instagram: www.instagram.com/celestehartwell/
Follow on Facebook: www.facebook.com/celestekhartwell
Chat on Clubhouse: www.clubhouse.com/@celestehartwell

KELLY NAGLE

Breaking Through Gender Barriers

I was a tomboy growing up. An outlier. Activities and interests normally designated as feminine didn't hold my attention as much as sports or action figures. In elementary school, while the girls congregated on the other side of the playground, I played sports with the boys. I remember an unspoken awkwardness about my presence on the kickball field at first. Even as kids we already had an awareness of gendered activities. To the boys' credit, however, I wasn't shunned; although at first, I was the last person picked to join a team. After a few weeks of proving my athletic skills, however, that changed.

I always had an affinity for sports and more male-associated activities. I remember spending Sundays watching football games. My brother and I collected baseball and basketball cards. We'd spend hours cataloging our cards, researching their worth and perusing statistics. For Christmas and birthdays, I asked my family for Starter jackets and my favorite teams' attire. Initially, there was some skepticism about my requesting the same gifts as my brother and male cousins; however, that eventually dissipated.

For much of my childhood, I was aware that my preferences for athletics and disinterest in most feminine-associated activities differed from my peers. At the time, though, I couldn't pinpoint why that was the case or where the underlying motivation stemmed from. I just knew I was going to pursue my interests. And the more people insisted that I do what was "normal," the more I resisted. As a child, I couldn't appreciate that had I been born just a couple decades earlier I may not have had the same latitude to follow the passions that led me beyond the boundaries of my gender.

By the time I was born, women had more options for their lives outside wife, mother, and a short list of professions. I grew up in a home where both my parents worked full time and had long, successful careers. My grandmothers talked about their experiences working in the corporate world. I heard stories of my great-aunt breaking barriers herself. She graduated from law school in the minority of women and had an impressive career. She was a partner in a law firm and served on the New Jersey Board of Higher Education and the Rutgers University Board of Governors. Her most inspiring accolade was leading the Board of Governors from 1973-1976 as the first female president.

I was always impressed hearing about my great-aunt's accomplishments as a child. However, I didn't appreciate their magnitude until I understood the obstacles women faced during her lifetime. Nor could I fully appreciate how her path towards pursuing her passions in a far more restrictive society would have been much more arduous than anything I would experience. I have a deep admiration for my great-aunt's tenacity, and I reflect on her success and life choices often.

As I grew up and stepped out of the small world of suburban Central Jersey, I became more aware of how my aspirations differed from my peers and society at large. From elementary through high school, I had come to be accepted for doing things my own way, but the realities of resisting gendered expectations caught up with me in and after college. None more so than my choice to not have children.

In college, when my female friends talked about their futures, it always included motherhood. I envisioned my future self hustling through a city in a pinstripe suit on my way to a corner office and traveling the world, either for leisure or for humanitarian-focused work. Raising a family never entered my consciousness. Being a mother is an important and fulfilling role for many women; I've just never aspired to it.

Thanks to women like Ruth Bader Ginsburg, I can make that choice and many others about my life without them affecting my livelihood. Although, as far as our society has come to accept and even expect women to want the same goals, jobs, and successes as a man, we have a hard time accepting women not fulfilling a contrived expectation of their gender. I may be generalizing in my observations, but I've come to this conclusion based on personal experience.

I'm always astonished that despite all of the advancements of women in society, I still deal with criticism about choosing not to be a mother. That criticism has lessened over the years. Perhaps because there are more women who have been brave enough to publicly share their same choice. Or because my childbearing years are almost behind me. Either way, every time I'm confronted with comments, like I'm "selfish" or "I'll change my mind" or "I'll regret my decision," I'm reminded of how far we still need to go in breaking through archaic gender expectations. Spoiler alert: I am blessed with having some amazing children in my life who bring me immense joy, including my boyfriend's son and daughter. No regrets here.

My own preferences for disregarding gender barriers and my great-aunt's legacy led me to take a keen interest in women's rights and gender-based violence. In graduate school, my research focused on breaking through the gendered lens of society and how, despite the legal advancements in gender equality, women are still restricted by the confines of patriarchy and culturally constructed ideas of feminism. It was during graduate school that I fell in love with RBG and began to understand the magnitude of her work on my own life.

Without RBG and other fearless and visionary women, like my great-aunt, I wouldn't have been able to follow my passions, regardless of my gender. I couldn't have been that young girl on the playground playing sports alongside the boys. Nor could I have envisioned a future where I would advance and thrive without depending on a man. Without RBG's work, I would have had to spend my youth learning important skills like ironing and sewing instead of a lay-up or crossover.

Although RBG's legal career is impressive in its own merit, her tenacity and refusal to give into "normal" expectations resonated with me the most. RBG was unapologetically authentic, regardless of whether her thoughts, actions, or mannerisms were popular or accepted. She was a brilliant woman who had a vision for a future that seemed unfathomable in her youth. Her convictions were so strong that she could blaze her own trail without faltering, despite roadblocks, challenges, and condescension. Throughout her career, she kept her composure and let her brilliance and skills quietly shine. Doing things her own way, even though they weren't the "norm," led to a highly successful life—both personally and professionally.

RBG's example drives my work today; the legal groundwork she laid allows me to turn my passion for creating a more equal and sustainable world into a reality. After spending years in the nonprofit sector, I founded two businesses: one to empower teens to advance social justice and the other to empower adults, particularly women, to rise as leaders and follow their own passions. It wasn't easy to start these endeavors. But unlike women in the past, I didn't have to worry about finding a male co-signer to open a business checking account, get a credit card, or start my business. Thanks, RBG!

As the co-founder of Teen Think Tank Project, I have the pleasure of working with socially conscious teenagers to research major social justice issues and create policy frameworks for change. These young men and women sit side-by-side, regardless of their gender, race, ethnicity, or socio-economic background, to tackle some of the most pressing injustices in our society. We look at each other as equals and strive to create a world that follows in that same vein.

These students embody RBG's vision for society and will continue her legacy of breaking down barriers. There's one impressive young woman from our program who always comes to mind when I think of our future leaders. She is a high school senior who is about to start a career of service to our country as an appointee at the United States Coast Guard Academy. Her dream is to be a female officer in the USCG. Although challenges still exist for women in the military, this amazing student has never worried about how her gender may limit her opportunities. She's optimistic that more women will rise as leaders so the military can be more representative of those who serve. And she's determined to help make that happen!

RBG's legacy is a reminder that following our vision, no matter how improbable it may seem at the time, can make a difference. Her legacy motivates me every day to try and have a positive impact on society. On the days when frustration and doubt creep in, I think about this diminutive woman who built her notoriety and success over decades. Her vision and unique personality immortalized her, despite being considered an outlier at the outset.

An altruist at heart, Kelly Nagle, M.A. Political Science – United Nations and Global Policy, is motivated by fighting for social justice and empowering others. After eleven years fundraising, advocating for health equity, and implementing community health programs in the nonprofit sector, Kelly followed her passions into the entrepreneurial world.

Kelly is the co-founder of *Teen Think Tank Project*, a student-run policy institute that develops policy frameworks for social justice issues and empowers students to become future changemakers.

She is also the founder of *Uncharted*. After emerging stronger, healthier, and happier from a devastating relationship, Kelly was motivated to help others find self-empowerment. Through *Uncharted* she helps clients build the skills to defy expectations and challenges and chart their own course to happiness.

Kelly holds an MA from Rutgers University in political science-United Nations and global policy and a BA in history from Loyola University Maryland.

Kelly lives in New Jersey and enjoys the love of her partner, Steve, and her dog, Penelope.

info@kellynagle.com
kellynagle.com
teenthinktankproject.com
www.linkedin.com/in/kellyenagle

JENNY GRACE MORRIS

Adopting New Viewpoints

When I heard people mention RBG, I thought, *The only things we have in common are we are both short, have a strong sense of justice, and love theater: she, opera; and I, Broadway musicals.* When I was cast as a reenactor in the role of Susan B. Anthony, I researched her history, along with modern-day supporters of women's rights, including our heroine, Ruth Bader Ginsburg. Among other things, I learned RBG stood for laws pertaining to all persons, but given only to men. Easy to envy as a brilliant woman, she also attracted a mensch (her husband, Martin D. Ginsburg), a true gentleman, who admired her intellect rather than being intimidated by it.

How could RBG have an effect on my life? Researching her many achievements, I realized her influence *did* contribute to my life experiences. There have been many wonderful benefits bestowed on my generation that I have taken for granted. Contrast this to women in the 1960s who tried to get credit, such as a home mortgage. Back then, banks required a woman to have her husband or another man cosign on a loan. A credit card in her own name would have been denied because she was female.

RBG promoted equal rights for both married and single women. Eventually, the Equal Credit Opportunity Act passed in 1974, allowing women to apply for credit cards and mortgages without a male cosigner. I can't imagine trusting a person, because of his gender, to cosign with me on anything, especially something as valuable as a mortgage, even if he was of good character, rich, and handsome. In those days, many customs pertained to married women, not single. Most women didn't have their own finances; marriage gave them financial security.

Women raising children did not usually work outside the home—many men did not encourage or want their wives to work. I ask, *Why would anyone with their own source of income give up their financial rights to walk down the aisle and say, "I do."?*

I have discovered cultural differences in men's views on women working. In my family, men were honored for providing well for their families; working wives reflected negatively on the man's ability to create adequate income. However, my friends' families expected that every member, regardless of gender, needed to work and contribute. Our family often discussed finances at the dinner table. By the time I was in elementary school, I could calculate a tip, but no one ever discussed my working or how to create independence without relying on a husband for my income. Today, if a male had to cosign for me to open a bank account, I know where my money would be stashed—under the mattress of an unused bed. (I am a bit of a princess and to put it under my own mattress would lead to uncomfortable sleeping conditions.)

I had dreamed of getting married but wasn't surprised it didn't happen. My biological father didn't want me to get married and my stepfather told me no one would marry me. So no pressure there! In retrospect, I can see marriage wasn't—isn't—a good fit for me because of all the domestic tasks involved. Cooking, cleaning, organizing, and then teaching my children how to do those chores would have proved disastrous. My success in the kitchen is limited to making chocolate chip cookies, which are delicious, but even those of us with a sweet tooth would find them tiresome at every meal.

One of RBG's influences on the world included equal pay for equal work. She created an atmosphere where being single became more popular than in earlier history—even if not by choice. Still, I wanted a family to love on, other than the usual friends, cats, or non-profits. In 2003, a friend of mine, confused about life decisions, asked me to pray for her. I prayed using words from our pastor. I heard a voice.

"What about your life?"

"What *about* my life?" I replied.

"You are going to adopt a little girl from Russia," the voice said.

"Don't you know I am single?"

"Yes, and what's your point?"

Before the 1970s, restrictions had prevented unmarried women from adopting. Even if a woman were wealthy, remained healthy, and could provide the child a loving home, no one would allow her to adopt. But adoption laws had changed by the 1990s and unmarried women were permitted to adopt. God knew that. I didn't.

Blessed by the women's movement, my mom and I traveled to Russia twice to adopt my daughter. I believe the changes in American law influenced women's rights in other countries as well. Russia required me, as the adoptive parent, to appear in court for a final judgment on my ability to raise my daughter. The female judge, who our agency had requested because she was lenient, approved my adoption. Raising a child by myself had challenges, but I'm grateful for the opportunity and for laws supporting a woman's right to adopt without a male partner.

My experience gained from parenthood led me to host international students over the years. Certain countries wouldn't allow their children to stay in a single-parent household, some needed approval from the child and their family. Happily, the USA saw the value of a young person's experience in a one-parent household. I still keep in touch with the students I hosted on a regular basis. They have no regrets having lived with just a mom in the US.

A woman's right to work and fair treatment of female employees have improved over the years. I appreciate the effects on my family, most of whom hadn't had opportunities in previous decades to be either an attorney, doctor, or federal judge, artist, writer, negotiators, editor-in-chief, or physician's assistant. I appreciate that some relatives were able to attend schools of higher education which hadn't before been open to female students. RBG had a great deal to do with making these changes possible.

RBG's ability to befriend someone with opposing views inspired me the most. I had always wanted to be a diplomat and am passionate about engaging in deep conversations with people unlike myself. I find it enlightening to hear the stories and practices of various traditions, to emphasize commonalities rather than criticize differences, to practice "love thy neighbor" as interfaith groups do. If we want peace in the world, it must start with expressing compassion, understanding, and knowledge regarding each other's cultural points of view. How? By getting to know someone whose life experience is dissimilar to our own.

I belong to interfaith communities. When I hear of hurtful or bad behaviors of any religious believers, I ask, *Aren't they missing the mark? Do they believe in an All-Loving Divine presence, like I do? I don't remember there being anything in treasured scriptures about unkind actions getting one closer to Supreme Love.* In my experience, most of us interested in interfaith gatherings strive to illustrate, through positive discussions, our commitment to human decency and acceptance. These groups understand it's not the religions themselves but rather individuals who choose to violate their own doctrinal teachings causing society to think the entire body of followers have wrathful intentions.

Conflicts in beliefs don't have to turn to hurtful and bad behavior. RBG and Antonin Scalia enjoyed a warm, faithful friendship *and* disagreed on the interpretation of the law. In spite of those differences, they admired each other and enjoyed the opera together. They could've purchased individual tickets on opposite ends of the theater, but their opposite ends were only as they voted. They respected each other and listened to one another's viewpoints, though they thought the other's views were incorrect. Like RBG, I relish my friends from both sides of the political spectrum. I believe we need critical thinkers, both conservative and liberal, but not thinkers that criticize. Now, when faced with someone holding the opposite viewpoint from mine, someone who I perceive as wearing dark sunglasses, I might ask more challenging questions; but I'm interested in their conclusion and why/how they came to it. RBG argued from her perspective and remained friends with those with whom she differed. I want to do the same by following in her footsteps. Ginsburg's ability to have good relationships with those with opposite viewpoints is a peaceful example of how we can present our ideas to those who disagree with us. Would it be fun or disastrous today to bring opposing thoughts together at a dinner party? I would hope it would be fun—we could call it, "The Ginsburg—Scalia Dinner."

The number of women whose lives have been influenced by the interpretation of law presented by RBG is vast. Our unique stories are impacted by different amendments, including an unmarried woman's right to adopt. If one doesn't agree with her policies, maybe they can appreciate the manner in which she led her life: with intelligence, grace, and persistence.

Jenny Grace Morris is an author, voice actor, clarity coach, and mom. She began writing when asked to create speeches, presentations, and workshops for conferences and international summits. She also emcees for events and co-hosts the monthly meeting *Write Your Book Right Now* for Gateway to Dreams. She created a blog called "Ask Amazing Grace" for an online news source called "Wilmington Faith and Values," which answered questions on faith and daily living. Though that news bureau no longer exists, the questions keep coming in, and so the blog continues.

Jenny's favorite activity is creating voices for characters in books, scripts, and copy.

askamazinggrace@gmail.com-coaching
jennygracemorris.com
jennygracevoiceacting@gmail.com-voice actor
JennyGraceMorris.icanvoice.com
www.facebook.com/jennygraceinspire
www.linkedin.com/in/jennygracemorris

BARBARA JOYCE

Allow and Trust the Process

In my research into women's rights in college in 1991, I set out to study the disparity of opportunities available to women in Osaka, Japan. I was curious to hear their complaints and discontent with the way women were treated in their country. I spoke to women employed at businesses and mothers who stayed at home with their children. What I found in my interviews of about twenty-five women was they were not unhappy or discontent at all. In fact, they were quite pleased with the state of affairs. They were grateful for their lives and the positions they held. My question to them was, "If given the opportunity, would you like to hold a different position?" Out of the twenty-five women, all of them sang the same receptive response, "We are quite happy the way things are."

I expected these women to be unhappy and unsettled with their lot in society—which was in direct contrast to the way I was raised and my beliefs about how society should be—instead, they were grateful.

As a woman who was brought up by a working mother passionate about women's issues and progressing their rights, any woman not wanting to have the same rights as men shocked me. I did not understand at the time how a woman would not want the same opportunities. As a naive undergraduate in 1991, that study opened my eyes to the many roles of women in the world. It opened my eyes also to the division of opinions concerning women's rights, abilities, and desires.

Worldwide roles and opinions have changed throughout my lifetime. What was true for women in 1991 is no longer true today. We are making headway in our culture and in our own lives at a rapid pace. And this forward movement does not come without its challenges.

You see, we are experiencing a global shift in equality and understanding, a rising global awareness and movement toward the freeing of women from the many faces of patriarchy and inequality. We are all being asked to look at our beliefs, circumstances, and behaviors in ways we have never dared to before. We, as humans, are being asked to level up to adapt to these rising new beliefs and circumstances. We are being driven by a higher definition of what equality means. We see this challenging many personal relationships as both men and women seek to find their rightful place in a new world of understanding—a new world brought about by many advocates. Susan B. Anthony, Mary Wollstonecraft, Elizabeth Cady Stanton, Alice Paul, Gloria Steinem, and Malala Yousafzai are a few women who come to mind when speaking of women's-rights activists. However, none have reached national and global notoriety at the level of the late Notorious RBG.

Ruth Bader Ginsburg lived a life of passion and purpose as she became the first tenured female professor at Columbia Law School in 1972. In 1980, President Jimmy Carter appointed her to the United States Court of Appeals for the District of Columbia. And in 1993, appointed by President Bill Clinton, she became the second woman to serve on the Supreme Court. Throughout her career, she continued to create change and to cement her legacy for making significant legal advances for women under the Equal Protection Clause of the Constitution. Among the many advances that would not be present in our society today without her influence, the greatest gift Ruth Bader Ginsburg gave the world was her example of looking within to find and to know the Truth inside each of us...and then living by it. Through her example, we see how a woman can come to know herself and to stay true to her own soulful path, no matter what the odds.

Justice Ginsburg, from a very early age, seemed to know herself and her path. Learning from her mother the importance of ideas and education, she found early on what she came here to do. She lived by some very important ideals, which she passed along as a legacy for us all to observe and learn from. Among the ideals she strove to attain: hard work, perseverance, exercise, and putting her family first, to name a few. She also knew and spoke often to the value of keeping a sense of humor, turning a deaf ear to harsh comments, crafting personal speech, and maintaining her own version of work-life balance. The hallmark trait that led her throughout her life, however, was the art of allowing her life to unfold and trusting the process.

Perhaps this art of allowing unfoldment happened initially, not as a matter of choice but as a matter of circumstance. RBG grew up during a time when women's rights and opportunities for education and employment in male-dominated professions was not easy or common to come by. She attended Cornell University, but did not go straight to law school immediately after graduation. She did not fret over this fact, but instead relished the joy of a new husband and new baby. Later, when the time unfolded, she attended Harvard Law School as one of nine women in a class of approximately 500. Trusting when timing was right, she transferred to Columbia Law School to keep the family together. She graduated at the top in her class. After graduation, even as valedictorian, she was unable to secure a job. In spite of that, RBG made a conscious choice to keep her chin up and to trust the next right thing would arise. And it did.

Ginsburg took a position as a research associate and associate director of the Columbia Law School Project on International Procedure where she learned Swedish and co-authored a book on civil procedure in Sweden. It was there she learned women could have a different lifestyle and legal position than what was observed in the United States. This led to the next position for Ginsburg, that of professor at Rutgers Law School and later at Columbia Law School where administration informed her she would be paid less than her male colleagues because her husband had a well-paying job. Being discriminated against at several points as she pursued her degree and her career led Justice Ginsburg to her purpose in life. She began her work in litigation and advocacy for equal rights.

Her brilliant mind and determination to help others who had experienced similar prejudices led to an uncanny ability to see the gaps in the law few others had seen previously. During this time, RBG co-founded the *Women's Rights Law Reporter* in 1970. In 1972, she co-founded the Women's Rights Project at ACLU (American Civil Liberties Union), where she served until her appointment to the Supreme Court. In working for these projects, she argued six gender-discrimination cases before the Supreme Court, winning five. In time, she became known as making significant legal advances for women under the Equal Protection Clause of the Constitution. This led to her confirmation on the DC Circuit Appeals

Court and her eventual nomination and confirmation as an associate justice on the Supreme Court. All along this path to her final position as Supreme Court justice, Ruth Bader Ginsburg allowed each event to unfold; she trusted each and every step in the process, staying steadfast to her aim.

It seems taking one step at a time and trusting that her life and purpose would unfold as it was meant to was something Justice Ginsburg effortlessly employed. But I know it did not come easily for her. She reached deep within to live with grit and gratitude for every single step along the way. Disappointment was, of course, part of the process, but she never let that get a chokehold on her. Instead, she took the situations by the lacey collar and made the best of them.

RBG's life could act as a template for how we can find our own Truth, our own purpose, and march faithfully forward, granting permission for the next step to unfold on our true path. RBG empowered us all with her words and actions to live a fulfilled and purposeful life, a life of true authenticity. One in which we make our mark.

So whatever endeavor you have going in your life, do not let any circumstance get you down. If you have found your purpose, stay true to it, taking one step at a time. We do not have a crystal ball to see how our futures will unfold. We do, however, know if we follow our passions and trust the process the next right thing will show up. When we live a life committed to our values and purpose, we live a life of growth and natural evolution.

So take it from the Notorious RBG and allow your life to unfold. And trust the process.

Barbara Joyce is a women's empowerment coach. Following her passion in personal development, she empowers women to find their voices and take steps in creating the lives they desire.

No stranger to failure and disappointment, Barbara realizes much of being a coach is about lifting the client up and creating an atmosphere of trust. By creating that atmosphere, Barbara helps women identify the pain points and obstacles that inhibit them. By addressing subconscious beliefs and habits, she helps clients expand who they are as individuals, create a stronger bond with what they already know to be true inside, and share their unique talents with the world. Barbara knows from personal experience that having that one person in life who we trust makes all the difference in the world. Barbara wants to be that person who guides her clients to freedom.

iambarbarajoyce@gmail.com
www.barbarajoyce.com/coaching/
www.facebook.com/barbarajoyce.me/?modal=admin_todo_tour
www.instagram.com/barbarajoycelive/
www.twitter.com/babsjoyce
www.linkedin.com/in/barbara-joyce-23601712/

CHRISTINE BLONN

When There Are Nine

The nomination of Ruth Bader Ginsburg went completely unnoticed by me. Of course, I was only twelve years old. I grew up surrounded by educated and working women. My friends' moms were scientists, lawyers, doctors, and business executives. My own mother held a successful career in marketing and advertising. As kids, we weren't just told we could do it all—i.e., go to college, have successful professional careers, and raise families—we were expected to.

I knew it wasn't easy. I saw my mom struggle. She took time off work when I was born and didn't go back until my younger brother was in preschool. She had a dazzling résumé, working for Fortune 500 companies before having children, but afterwards, she had a hard time finding a suitable job. She later joined an advertising agency full-time. As a working mother, while successful, the opportunities she had received as a single woman never came.

The 2000 election of George W. Bush, followed by September 11, 2001, the Iraq War, and the growing partisan divide broke my political complacency. I became aware. The court moved further to the right under President Bush. As the Supreme Court leaned toward conservatism, landmark cases affected everything from campaign finance laws to reproductive rights. As a liberal, I felt we were losing the battles. Politics suddenly became very personal.

The election of our first black president in 2008 was an epic moment in time. It seems like a dream—we were so hopeful, so sure it meant real change. But while a huge step forward, the backlash was swift and brutal.

Ruth Bader Ginsburg became my personal hero during this time. Or as I call her, the "Notorious RBG." Considered a moderate justice at her appointment in

1993, she was a whip-smart warrior with lace collars and oversized glasses fighting for the rights of women and minorities. Under President Bush, as the court leaned right, RBG leaned left and wrote dissenting votes. She was fighting for me.

The conservative/liberal battles in the Supreme Court became more personal to me when I became pregnant. My difficult pregnancy was made more difficult by a work environment that did not support a pregnant woman, a new mother, or even a mother with small children. I was exhausted and sick my entire first and second trimesters. I took anti-nausea medication, which didn't help the nausea but kept me from throwing up. It also made me light-headed. I fell asleep almost every night at seven or eight p.m. and spent mornings before work lying on the bathroom floor too sick to move. I slept through the weekends while my husband and family worked to get the house ready for the baby. I was privileged. I had a loving and supporting husband who earned a good income and had health insurance. I had family nearby who helped around the house. But I was also frustrated—frustrated with the law and lack of support for working moms (even moms-to-be).

Like approximately forty percent of the workforce at the time, I did not qualify for the twelve weeks' (unpaid) maternity leave promised in the Family Medical Leave Act (FMLA), which went into effect in 1993, just five days before RBG was sworn in as a US Supreme Court Justice. I did not qualify for FMLA leave because I worked for a small, private organization; therefore, the only leave offered to me was six weeks for a vaginal birth or eight weeks for a c-section. I was frustrated that my employer balked at the time I took off for excessive morning sickness, including a three-day hospital stay; frustrated they did not want to have my position empty for six to eight weeks or to have a temp in my place during my time off; frustrated they did not want to deal with the practicalities of a new working mother. They made it very clear they did not want me back after I had my baby.

After calculating my income versus the cost of daycare, I realized I would make only about forty-two cents an hour. At that price, I knew I didn't want to return to work and to what I then considered a hostile working environment. While financially difficult, I had the luxury to choose to stay home with my baby. I gave myself permission to quit.

Before leaving work, I hired an assistant who wanted my job, and my boss did not want to deal with my "situation." I negotiated. I told my boss I would not return after childbirth, but I would be allowed to stay until then; and in return I would keep my same health insurance to pay for the birth and get my short-term disability insurance payment for the six to eight weeks afterward. So I stayed and helped train my replacement before going into labor almost a month early.

It wasn't until several years later when I went to a "mommy dinner" organized by my church that I realized how common my experience was. One workplace told a woman she went to the bathroom too much because of her morning sickness and needed to throw up in her trash can; other new mothers had to pump breast milk in their desk chairs or in uncleaned bathrooms. Some women talked about the challenge of going back to work exhausted, and all talked about the expense of childcare. We were privileged, white, affluent, educated, professional women; and yet we all had stories about discrimination and harassment. And if this is what we faced, what did women with less privilege and support have to withstand and tolerate? We were all living in a world where two incomes were a necessity for most families but in a society and culture that made no allowances for the needs of working parents.

So how does this change now that the Notorious RBG is gone? To me, the best way to honor Ruth Bader Ginsburg is to keep working and fighting for equality. As much progress as she made, there is still far to go and her legacy is our continued fight. In her own words:

...I spoke of great changes I have seen in women's occupations. Yet one must acknowledge the still bleak part of the picture. Most people in poverty in the United States and the world over are women and children, women's earnings here and abroad trail the earnings of men with compatible education and experience, our workplaces do not adequately accommodate the demands of childbearing and child rearing, and yet we have yet to devise effective ways to ward off sexual harassment at work and domestic violence in our homes. I am optimistic, however, that the movement toward enlistment of the talent of all who compose "We, the people," will continue.[10]

---

10 Ruth Bader Ginsburg, *The New York Times*, "Ruth Bader Ginsburg's Advice for Living, Oct 1, 2016, accessed June 9, 2021, https://www.nytimes.com/2016/10/02/opinion/sunday/ruth-bader-ginsburgs-advice-for-living.html

As our country and the world start to come out of a year of a global pandemic, the fight becomes essential when we consider the shutdown of schools and childcare facilities which hit women especially hard. Some women sacrificed their careers to become full-time educators for their children at home with distance-learning; others had to watch their children struggle because they could not financially afford to take extended time off work, and most, unfortunately, lost incomes as well as child support.

My hope is that we can take the lessons not only of RBG's legal work but her personal life to help us heal. Her marriage to Martin D. Ginsburg shows the importance of a supporting spouse and is a model for an equal and loving partnership. Ruth Bader Ginsburg acknowledged that she would not have been appointed to the Supreme Court without her husband's support. And her astounding friendship with conservative Supreme Court Justice Anthony Scalia demonstrates the ability of two people with seemly diametrically opposed opinions to work together with mutual respect and civility. If only the other branches of government could work together in the way that RBG and Scalia did.

I remember in my high school debate class, I had to argue in favor of feminism. I argued that feminism was the belief that men and women were equal and should be treated as equals. While my classmates agreed with the concept, they still looked at the word "feminist" as a dirty word. I hope that is no longer the case.

Women like Ruth Bader Ginsburg have shown us that women can be feminists, career women, wives, and mothers. We are free to define ourselves as we wish. So we will willingly pick up Ruth Bader Ginsburg's sword and keep fighting. Fighting and working to remake the world as a safer, better place for our daughters.

Ruth Bader Ginsburg notoriously said, "People ask me sometimes…'When will there be enough women on the court?' And my answer is: 'When there are nine.'"

We will know we've won when we no longer have to ask, "How many women is enough?"

As a marketing professional for over ten years, Christine Blonn's experience includes working for the Arts and Education Council of Greater St. Louis as a marketing consultant and for Chicago's primary Public Broadcasting Station, WTTW, as a marketing project manager. During her career, she successfully managed the creation, development, production, and analysis of direct, promotional, and digital marketing campaigns. In addition, she managed multiple marketing communication channels, including direct mail, email, and sweepstakes promotions for brands such as Secret Deodorant, Old Spice, Olay, and Noxzema.

Christine holds both a bachelor of arts degree in English and history and a master's degree in communication, specializing in journalism from Marquette University.

Christine and husband, Phil, welcomed their first child in 2013, a daughter named "Sophie." In her free time, she loves cooking, reading, traveling, watching old movies, and, most importantly, spending time with her family.

twitter.com/cmblonn
www.facebook.com/christine.blonn
www.instagram.com/cmblonn/

Afterword

Why Can't I?

By birth order I was second
But actually, second to none
Because I was chosen for 9 years
To act as Dad's "stand-in-son."

     Help carry my hammer, honey.
My tom girl self tagged right along.
I aspired to do what boys got to do.
And I thought nothing at all was wrong.

<u>Why</u> can't I be a patrol boy—uh…patrol girl?
I asked my teachers at school.
     Only boys are wise and strong enough.
     You know that is the rule.

Well, then—<u>why</u> can't I be an altar boy,
I mean—altar girl instead?
     That's not allowed either, child.
     Get those silly ideas out of your head.

Okay. I really want to play soccer.
     No, that's a rough sport for boys.
     And don't ask again for trucks and tanks.
     Go play with pretty girl toys.

I want to drop my typing class.
     OK… but it's important all girls can.
     'Cause if you don't find a husband,
     Secretary work is your back-up plan.

Years later, I <u>needed</u> typing—
For writing books and getting my Ph.D.

Continued on next page

Why didn't they advise me in high school,
How inconvenient not typing would be?

In my twenties as a female token,
A federal court employee,
    I was judged by standards higher
    Than male colleagues—constantly.
    They pulled porn magazines from desk drawers.
    And kicked holes through walls in a fit.
    They plucked my bra shouting," Robin Hood!"
    Those overgrown "boys" never quit!
    Male co-workers were advanced ahead of me.
    You're less qualified, they'd say.

But <u>why</u> can't I be promoted over the guys?
More credentials line my resume.
Married and yet child free—

And still treated like a tart.

    More sexual harassment edged in:
    Jump on the table—we'll give you a start.

My initiatives and questions were relegated
To the bottom of the circular file.
    You're abrasive and insubordinate!
    Now where's that girlie smile?

It came down to the seven-year battle—
In federal appeals court I'd finally win
One victory against the system.
On record was the court's own sin.

And if I knew then what I know now,
Would I do it over? Endure all the stress?
Would I still pay big bucks to my lawyer?
Seeing my daughters, I can say—yes!

Made in the USA
Monee, IL
09 July 2021

72420595R00069